LIGHT FOR MY PATH

LIGHT FOR MY PATH

ILLUMINATING SELECTIONS FROM SCRIPTURE

BARBOUR
PUBLISHING

Contents

*T*hy word is a lamp unto my feet,
and a light unto my path.
PSALM 119:105

Whatever the need of the moment, the answer is to be found in scripture, if we take the time to search for it. Whatever we're feeling, whatever we're suffering, whatever we're hoping—the Bible has something to say to us.

This collection of scriptures is meant for use as a handy reference when you need the Bible's guidance on a particular problem in your life. Of course, the Bible is a very large book, and all of its topics—as numerous as the many facets of your life—may not be covered here. In-depth personal study of the Bible is always the best method for grasping the great truths of the scriptures.

But if you're feeling especially lonely or afraid, or if you're wondering what God has to say about salvation, faith, pride, or parenting, some of the Bible's wisdom and comfort is available to you here, collected by topic. The topics are arranged alphabetically for ease of use.

The Bible is God's road map for life. May this book help you find light for your path.

Anger

Dear God, sometimes I get angry so easily. Things go wrong, people don't act the way I want them to, someone's words rub me the wrong way. Help me, Father, to control my anger, to keep it from spilling out, hurting those around me. Remind me that usually, when it comes right down to it, I'm angry simply because I can't have my own way. Give me the strength to accept whatever You send into my life. Amen.

A God ready to pardon, gracious and merciful, slow to anger, and of great kindness.

NEHEMIAH 9:17

The LORD is gracious, and full of compassion; slow to anger, and of great mercy.

PSALM 145:8

h eat not a furnace for your foe so hot
That it do singe yourself.
—WILLIAM SHAKESPEARE

For his anger endureth but a moment; in his favour is life: weeping may endure for a night, but joy cometh in the morning.

PSALM 30:5

Wherefore, my beloved brethren, let every man be swift to hear, slow to speak, slow to wrath:

For the wrath of man worketh not the righteousness of God.

JAMES 1:19–20

Be not hasty in thy spirit to be angry: for anger resteth in the bosom of fools.

ECCLESIASTES 7:9

He that is soon angry dealeth foolishly.

PROVERBS 14:17

A wrathful man stirreth up strife: but he that is slow to anger appeaseth strife.

PROVERBS 15:18

An angry man stirreth up strife, and a furious man aboundeth in transgression.

PROVERBS 29:22

Make no friendship with an angry man; and with a furious man thou shalt not go:

Lest thou learn his ways, and get a snare to thy soul.

PROVERBS 22:24–25

Cease from anger, and forsake wrath: fret not thyself in any wise to do evil.

PSALM 37:8

He that is slow to anger is better than the mighty; and he that ruleth his spirit than he that taketh a city.

PROVERBS 16:32

A soft answer turneth away wrath: but grievous words stir up anger.

PROVERBS 15:1

Fathers, provoke not your children to anger, lest they be discouraged.

COLOSSIANS 3:21

Be ye angry, and sin not: let not the sun go down upon your wrath.

EPHESIANS 4:26

The discretion of a man deferreth his anger; and it is his glory to pass over a transgression.

PROVERBS 19:11

It is better to dwell in the wilderness, than with a contentious and an angry woman.

PROVERBS 21:19

But I say unto you, That whosoever is angry with his brother without a cause shall be in danger of the judgment.

MATTHEW 5:22

But now ye also put off all these; anger, wrath, malice, blasphemy, filthy communication out of your mouth.

COLOSSIANS 3:8

Let all bitterness, and wrath, and anger, and clamour, and evil speaking, be put away from you, with all malice:
And be ye kind one to another, tenderhearted, forgiving one another, even as God for Christ's sake hath forgiven you.

EPHESIANS 4:31–32

Wrath is cruel, and anger is outrageous; but who is able to stand before envy?

PROVERBS 27:4

Dearly beloved, avenge not yourselves, but rather give place unto wrath: for it is written, Vengeance is mine; I will repay, saith the Lord.

Therefore if thine enemy hunger, feed him; if he thirst, give him drink: for in so doing thou shalt heap coals of fire on his head.

Be not overcome of evil, but overcome evil with good.

ROMANS 12:19–21

As long as anger lives,
she continues to be the fruitful mother
of many unhappy children.
—JOHN CLIMACUS

If thine enemy be hungry, give him bread to eat; and if he be thirsty, give him water to drink:

For thou shalt heap coals of fire upon his head, and the LORD shall reward thee.

PROVERBS 25:21–22

Belief

Lord, in a world where we've learned to rely only on what we can perceive with our five senses, sometimes we can't help but be filled with doubts. After all, we can't see Your face or hear Your voice or touch Your hand. And meanwhile, the world bombards us with messages that contradict our belief in You and Your kingdom. Despite all that, though, Father, give us the strength to believe. Amen.

For God so loved the world, that he gave his only begotten Son, that whosoever believeth in him should not perish, but have everlasting life.

JOHN 3:16

To him give all the prophets witness, that through his name whosoever believeth in him shall receive remission of sins.

ACTS 10:43

As it is written, Behold, I lay in Sion a stumblingstone and rock of offence: and whosoever believeth on him shall not be ashamed.

ROMANS 9:33

But as many as received him, to them gave he power to become the sons of God, even to them that believe on his name.

JOHN 1:12

He that believeth on him is not condemned: but he that believeth not is condemned already, because he hath not believed in the name of the only begotten Son of God.

JOHN 3:18

He that believeth on the Son hath everlasting life: and he that believeth not the Son shall not see life; but the wrath of God abideth on him.

JOHN 3:36

Jesus said unto him, If thou canst believe, all things are possible to him that believeth.

MARK 9:23

Verily, verily, I say unto you, He that believeth on me hath everlasting life.

JOHN 6:47

Wherefore also it is contained in the scripture, Behold, I lay in Sion a chief corner stone, elect, precious: and he that believeth on him shall not be confounded.

1 PETER 2:6

And they said, Believe on the Lord Jesus Christ, and thou shalt be saved, and thy house.

ACTS 16:31

Understanding is the reward of faith. Therefore seek not understanding that thou mayest believe, but believe that thou mayest understand.
—AUGUSTINE (c. 416)

I am come a light into the world, that whosoever believeth on me should not abide in darkness.

JOHN 12:4

And Jesus said unto them, I am the bread of life: he that cometh to me shall never hunger; and he that believeth on me shall never thirst.

JOHN 6:35

Jesus saith unto him, Thomas, because thou hast seen me, thou hast believed: blessed are they that have not seen, and yet have believed.

JOHN 20:29

Hear me, O Judah, and ye inhabitants of Jerusalem; Believe in the LORD your God, so shall ye be established; believe his prophets, so shall ye prosper.

2 CHRONICLES 20:20

Ye are my witnesses, saith the LORD, and my servant whom I have chosen: that ye may know and believe me, and understand that I am he: before me there was no God formed, neither shall there be after me.

ISAIAH 43:10

And this is his commandment, That we should believe on the name of his Son Jesus Christ, and love one another, as he gave us commandment.

1 JOHN 3:23

Charity

*Jesus, remind me that when I give to others, I am
really giving to You. Help me to share all that You
have given me—my money, my possessions, my time,
my talents, my love—with those who are in need. Amen.*

But when thou makest a feast, call the poor, the maimed, the lame, the blind:

And thou shalt be blessed; for they cannot recompense thee: for thou shalt be recompensed at the resurrection of the just.

LUKE 14:13–14

He that despiseth his neighbour sinneth: but he that hath mercy on the poor, happy is he.

PROVERBS 14:21

Blessed is he that considereth the poor: the LORD will deliver him in time of trouble.

The LORD will preserve him, and keep him alive; and he shall be blessed upon the earth: and thou wilt not deliver him unto the will of his enemies.

PSALM 41:1–2

Give, and it shall be given unto you; good measure, pressed down, and shaken together, and running over, shall men give into your bosom. For with the same measure that ye mete withal it shall be measured to you again.

LUKE 6:38

Sell that ye have, and give alms; provide yourselves bags which wax not old, a treasure in the heavens that faileth not, where no thief approacheth, neither moth corrupteth.

LUKE 12:33

He hath dispersed, he hath given to the poor; his righteousness endureth for ever; his horn shall be exalted with honour.

PSALM 112:9

He that giveth unto the poor shall not lack: but he that hideth his eyes shall have many a curse.

PROVERBS 28:27

The biggest disease today is not leprosy or tuberculosis, but rather the feeling of being unwanted, uncared for and deserted by everybody. The greatest evil is the lack of love and charity.
—MOTHER TERESA

And if thou draw out thy soul to the hungry, and satisfy the afflicted soul; then shall thy light rise in obscurity, and thy darkness be as the noonday.

ISAIAH 58:10

Every man according as he purposeth in his heart, so let him give; not grudgingly, or of necessity: for God loveth a cheerful giver.

2 CORINTHIANS 9:7

There is that scattereth, and yet increaseth; and there is that withholdeth more than is meet, but it tendeth to poverty.

The liberal soul shall be made fat: and he that watereth shall be watered also himself.

PROVERBS 11:24–25

Charge them that are rich in this world, that they be not highminded, nor trust in uncertain riches, but in the living God, who giveth us richly all things to enjoy;

That they do good, that they be rich in good works, ready to distribute, willing to communicate.

1 Timothy 6:17–18

Heal the sick, cleanse the lepers, raise the dead, cast out devils: freely ye have received, freely give.

Matthew 10:8

I have shewed you all things, how that so labouring ye ought to support the weak, and to remember the words of the Lord Jesus, how he said, It is more blessed to give than to receive.

Acts 20:35

He that hath pity upon the poor lendeth unto the Lord; and that which he hath given will he pay him again.

Proverbs 19:17

Cast thy bread upon the waters: for thou shalt find it after many days.

Ecclesiastes 11:1

He is ever merciful, and lendeth; and his seed is blessed.

PSALM 37:26

Is it not to deal thy bread to the hungry, and that thou bring the poor that are cast out to thy house? when thou seest the naked, that thou cover him; and that thou hide not thyself from thine own flesh?

Then shall thy light break forth as the morning, and thine health shall spring forth speedily: and thy righteousness shall go before thee; the glory of the LORD shall be thy rereward.

ISAIAH 58:7–8

Then shall the King say unto them on his right hand, Come, ye blessed of my Father, inherit the kingdom prepared for you from the foundation of the world:

For I was an hungered, and ye gave me meat: I was thirsty, and ye gave me drink: I was a stranger, and ye took me in:

Naked, and ye clothed me: I was sick, and ye visited me: I was in prison, and ye came unto me.

Then shall the righteous answer him, saying, Lord, when saw we thee an hungered, and fed thee? or thirsty, and gave thee drink?

When saw we thee a stranger, and took thee in? or naked, and clothed thee?

Or when saw we thee sick, or in prison, and came unto thee?

And the King shall answer and say unto them, Verily I say unto you, Inasmuch as ye have done it unto one of the least of these my brethren, ye have done it unto me.

MATTHEW 25:34–40

And the Levite, (because he hath no part nor inheritance with thee,) and the stranger, and the fatherless, and the widow, which are within thy gates, shall come, and shall eat and be satisfied; that the LORD thy God may bless thee in all the work of thine hand which thou doest.

DEUTERONOMY 14:29

Universal and constant usefulness to all, is the important lesson. And when we are fully and wholly given up to the Lord, I am sure the heart can long for nothing so much as that our time, talents, life, soul, and spirit, may be upon earth a constant and living sacrifice.
—LADY HUNTINGTON IN A LETTER TO JOHN WESLEY

Then Jesus beholding him loved him, and said unto him, One thing thou lackest: go thy way, sell whatsoever thou hast, and give to the poor, and thou shalt have treasure in heaven: and come, take up the cross, and follow me.

MARK 10:21

Comfort

*Thank You, Jesus, that Your Spirit brings
such comfort to my heart. When I am sad
or frightened, remind me that all I need to do
is open myself to You—and Your love will wrap
around me like a warm, comforting blanket. Amen.*

God is our refuge and strength, a very present help in trouble.

Therefore will not we fear, though the earth be removed, and though the mountains be carried into the midst of the sea;

Though the waters thereof roar and be troubled, though the mountains shake with the swelling thereof.

PSALM 46:1–3

Though I walk in the midst of trouble, thou wilt revive me: thou shalt stretch forth thine hand against the wrath of mine enemies, and thy right hand shall save me.

PSALM 138:7

The LORD is my rock, and my fortress, and my deliverer; my God, my strength, in whom I will trust; my buckler, and the horn of my salvation, and my high tower.

PSALM 18:2

For he hath not despised nor abhorred the affliction of the afflicted; neither hath he hid his face from him; but when he cried unto him, he heard.

PSALM 22:24

Though he fall, he shall not be utterly cast down: for the LORD upholdeth him with his hand.

PSALM 37:24

These things I have spoken unto you, that in me ye might have peace. In the world ye shall have tribulation: but be of good cheer; I have overcome the world.

JOHN 16:33

The LORD is good, a strong hold in the day of trouble;
and he knoweth them that trust in him.

NAHUM 1:7

Whatsoever I can desire or imagine
for my comfort: I look for it not here,
but hereafter. For if I might alone have all
the comforts of the world and enjoy all its
delights: it is certain that they could
not long endure.
—THOMAS Á KEMPIS

But the salvation of the righteous is of the LORD: he is
their strength in the time of trouble.

PSALM 37:39

Cast thy burden upon the LORD, and he shall sustain
thee: he shall never suffer the righteous to be moved.

PSALM 55:22

Come unto me, all ye that labour and are heavy laden,
and I will give you rest.

MATTHEW 11:28

Blessed be God, even the Father of our Lord Jesus Christ,
the Father of mercies, and the God of all comfort;

Who comforteth us in all our tribulation, that we may be able to comfort them which are in any trouble, by the comfort wherewith we ourselves are comforted of God.

For as the sufferings of Christ abound in us, so our consolation also aboundeth by Christ.

2 CORINTHIANS 1:3–5

For the Lord will not cast off for ever:

But though he cause grief, yet will he have compassion according to the multitude of his mercies.

For he doth not afflict willingly nor grieve the children of men.

LAMENTATIONS 3:31–33

Wait on the LORD: be of good courage, and he shall strengthen thine heart: wait, I say, on the LORD.

PSALM 27:14

The LORD also will be a refuge for the oppressed, a refuge in times of trouble.

PSALM 9:9

For I reckon that the sufferings of this present time are not worthy to be compared with the glory which shall be revealed in us.

ROMANS 8:18

Fear thou not; for I am with thee: be not dismayed; for I am thy God: I will strengthen thee; yea, I will help thee; yea, I will uphold thee with the right hand of my righteousness.

ISAIAH 41:10

The spirit of the Lord God is upon me; because the Lord hath anointed me to preach good tidings unto the meek; he hath sent me to bind up the brokenhearted, to proclaim liberty to the captives, and the opening of the prison to them that are bound.

ISAIAH 61:1

Let not your heart be troubled: ye believe in God, believe also in me.

JOHN 14:1

Earth has no sorrow
that Heaven cannot heal.
—THOMAS MORE

I, even I, am he that comforteth you: who art thou, that thou shouldest be afraid of a man that shall die, and of the son of man which shall be made as grass.

ISAIAH 51:12

As one whom his mother comforteth, so will I comfort you; and ye shall be comforted in Jerusalem.

ISAIAH 66:13

Contentment

*Dear Lord, thank You for the happiness
You bring to my life. Help me to find my
contentment in You and all that You have
given me. Amen.*

A merry heart doeth good like a medicine: but a broken spirit drieth the bones.

PROVERBS 17:22

Let your conversation be without covetousness; and be content with such things as ye have: for he hath said, I will never leave thee, nor forsake thee.

HEBREWS 13:5

All the days of the afflicted are evil: but he that is of a merry heart hath a continual feast.

PROVERBS 15:15

*T*rue contentment is a real, even
an active virtue—not only affirmative
but creative. It is the power of getting out
of any situation all there is in it.
—G.K. CHESTERTON

A sound heart is the life of the flesh: but envy the rottenness of the bones.

PROVERBS 14:30

But godliness with contentment is great gain.

1 TIMOTHY 6:6

Let not thine heart envy sinners: but be thou in the fear
of the LORD all the day long.

For surely there is an end; and thine expectation shall
not be cut off.

PROVERBS 23:17–18

And the soldiers likewise demanded of him, saying, And
what shall we do? And he said unto them, Do violence
to no man, neither accuse any falsely; and be content
with your wages.

LUKE 3:14

Not that I speak in respect of want: for I have learned, in
whatsoever state I am, therewith to be content.

PHILIPPIANS 4:11

Happy is he that hath the God of Jacob for his help,
whose hope is in the LORD his God.

PSALM 146:5

Happy is that people, that is in such a case: yea, happy is
that people, whose God is the LORD.

PSALM 144:15

CORRECTION, God's

Sometimes, God, Christians make You sound as though You're a stern, joyless taskmaster, waiting to bang us on the head if we so much as color outside the lines. Remind me, Jesus, that this image of the Father is a lie. Thank You that God is a loving parent who always wants the best for me; if You say "no," I know it's only because You want something far better for me. Help me to see Your love even in Your correction. Amen.

For which cause we faint not; but though our outward man perish, yet the inward man is renewed day by day.

For our light affliction, which is but for a moment, worketh for us a far more exceeding and eternal weight of glory.

2 CORINTHIANS 4:16–17

Thou shalt also consider in thine heart, that, as a man chasteneth his son, so the LORD thy God chasteneth thee.

DEUTERONOMY 8:5

Our Lord did not ask us to give up
the things of earth, but to exchange them
for better things.
—FULTON J. SHEEN

Behold, happy is the man whom God correcteth: therefore despise not thou the chastening of the Almighty:

For he maketh sore, and bindeth up: he woundeth, and his hands make whole.

JOB 5:17–18

For whom the LORD loveth he correcteth; even as a father the son in whom he delighteth.

PROVERBS 3:12

Blessed is the man whom thou the chastenest, O Lord, and teachest him out of thy law;

That thou mayest give him rest from the days of adversity, until the pit be digged for the wicked.

PSALM 94:12–13

For they verily for a few days chastened us after their own pleasure; but he for our profit, that we might be partakers of his holiness.

Now no chastening for the present seemeth to be joyous, but grievous: nevertheless afterward it yieldeth the peaceable fruit of righteousness unto them which are exercised thereby.

HEBREWS 12:10–11

Why do we say no?
In order to say yes to what really matters.
—MIRIAM ADENEY

For whom the Lord loveth he chasteneth, and scourgeth every son whom he receiveth.

If ye endure chastening, God dealeth with you as with sons; for what son is he whom the father chasteneth not?

HEBREWS 12:6–7

Duties to Our Parents

Thank You for my parents, God. Even though I'm grown up now, may my relationship with them continue to grow. Heal the old hurts and resentments with Your Holy Spirit. Thank You for all You've given me through these two people—and help me never be too busy to show them how much I love them. Amen.

Children, obey your parents in the Lord: for this is right.

Honour thy father and mother; which is the first commandment with promise;

That it may be well with thee, and thou mayest live long on the earth.

EPHESIANS 6:1–3

We don't have choices about who our parents are and how they treated us, but we have a choice about whether we forgive our parents and heal ourselves.

—BERNIE SIEGEL

Children, obey your parents in all things: for this is well pleasing unto the Lord.

COLOSSIANS 3:20

Thou knowest the commandments, Do not commit adultery, Do not kill, Do not steal, Do not bear false witness, Honour thy father and thy mother.

LUKE 18:20

Cursed be he that setteth light by his father or his mother. And all the people shall say, Amen.

DEUTERONOMY 27:16

Ye shall fear every man his mother, and his father, and

keep my sabbaths: I am the LORD your God.

LEVITICUS 19:3

Honour thy father and thy mother, as the LORD thy God hath commanded thee; that thy days may be prolonged, and that it may go well with thee, in the land which the LORD thy God giveth thee.

DEUTERONOMY 5:16

My son, keep thy father's commandment, and forsake not the law of thy mother.

PROVERBS 6:20

A wise son heareth his father's instruction: but a scorner heareth not rebuke.

PROVERBS 13:1

A fool despiseth his father's instruction: but he that regardeth reproof is prudent.

PROVERBS 15:5

Even a child is known by his doings, whether his work be pure, and whether it be right.

PROVERBS 20:11

The proverbs of Solomon. A wise son maketh a glad father: but a foolish son is the heaviness of his mother.

PROVERBS 10:1

Whoso keepeth the law is a wise son: but he that is a companion of riotous men shameth his father.

PROVERBS 28:7

From the loving example of one family
a whole state becomes loving.
—The Great Learning (c. 500 b.c.)

Now therefore hearken unto me, O ye children: for blessed are they that keep my ways.

Hear instruction, and be wise, and refuse it not.

Proverbs 8:32–33

Hearken unto thy father that begat thee, and despise not thy mother when she is old.

The father of the righteous shall greatly rejoice: and he that begetteth a wise child shall have joy of him.

Thy father and thy mother shall be glad, and she that bare thee shall rejoice.

My son, give me thine heart, and let thine eyes observe my ways.

Proverbs 23:22, 24–26

Eternal Life

*Remind me, Father, that my home is not
in this world but in eternity. Thank You that I am
already an inhabitant of Your eternal world. Amen.*

For the Lord himself shall descend from heaven with a shout, with the voice of the archangel, and with the trump of God: and the dead in Christ shall rise first.

1 Thessalonians 4:16

Verily, verily, I say unto you, He that believeth on me hath everlasting life.

John 6:47

he who binds to himself a joy
Does the wingéd life destroy;
But he who kisses the joy as it flies
Lives in eternity's sun rise.
—William Blake

Jesus said unto her, I am the resurrection, and the life: he that believeth in me, though he were dead, yet shall he live:

And whosoever liveth and believeth in me shall never die. Believest thou this?

John 11:25–26

And this is the promise that he hath promised us, even eternal life.

1 John 2:25

But let me tell you a wonderful secret God has revealed to

us. Not all of us will die, but we will all be transformed. It will happen in a moment, in the blinking of an eye, when the last trumpet is blown. For when the trumpet sounds, the Christians who have died will be raised with transformed bodies. And then we who are living will be transformed so that we will never die. For our perishable earthly bodies must be transformed into heavenly bodies that will never die.

When this happens—when our perishable earthly bodies have been transformed into heavenly bodies that will never die—then at last Scripture will come true:

> "Death is swallowed up in victory.
> O death, where is your victory?
> O death where is your sting?"

1 CORINTHIANS 15:51–55 NLT

Marvel not at this: for the hour is coming, in the which all that are in the graves shall hear his voice,

And shall come forth; they that have done good, unto the resurrection of life; and they that have done evil, unto the resurrection of damnation.

JOHN 5:28–29

And this is the record, that God hath given to us eternal life, and this life is in his Son.

These things have I written unto you that believe on the name of the Son of God; that ye may know that ye have eternal life, and that ye may believe on the name of the Son of God.

1 JOHN 5:11, 13

Therefore are they before the throne of God, and serve him day and night in his temple: and he that sitteth on the throne shall dwell among them.

They shall hunger no more, neither thirst any more; neither shall the sun light on them, nor any heat.

For the Lamb which is in the midst of the throne shall feed them, and shall lead them unto living fountains of waters: and God shall wipe away all tears from their eyes.

REVELATION 7:15–17

For God so loved the world, that he gave his only begotten Son, that whosoever believeth in him should not perish, but have everlasting life.

JOHN 3:16

In my Father's house are many mansions: if it were not so, I would have told you. I go to prepare a place for you.

And if I go and prepare a place for you, I will come again.

JOHN 14:2–3

The Spirit of God, who raised Jesus from the dead, lives in you. And just as he raised Christ from the dead, he will give life to your mortal body by this same Spirit living within you.

ROMANS 8:11 NLT

For we know that if our earthly house of this tabernacle were dissolved, we have a building of God, an house not made with hands, eternal in the heavens.

2 CORINTHIANS 5:1

So also is the resurrection of the dead. It is sown in corruption; it is raised in incorruption:

It is sown in dishonour; it is raised in glory: it is sown in weakness; it is raised in power:

It is sown a natural body; it is raised a spiritual body. There is a natural body, and there is a spiritual body.

1 CORINTHIANS 15:42–44

Eternal life is not a life for the future.
By charity we start eternity right here below.
—HENRI DE LUBAC

And God shall wipe away all tears from their eyes; and there shall be no more death, neither sorrow, nor crying, neither shall there be any more pain: for the former things are passed away.

REVELATION 21:4

And many of them that sleep in the dust of the earth shall awake, some to everlasting life, and some to shame and everlasting contempt.

DANIEL 12:2

For the wages of sin is death; but the gift of God is eternal life through Jesus Christ our Lord.

ROMANS 6:23

Faith

*Thank You, Jesus, that faith is not an emotion
that I need to work up inside of me. Instead, it is a gift
You give to me as I commit myself to You.
Help me to grow in faith. Amen.*

Now faith is the substance of things hoped for, the evidence of things not seen.

HEBREWS 11:1

Watch ye, stand fast in the faith, quit you like men, be strong.

1 CORINTHIANS 16:13

For by grace are ye saved through faith; and that not of yourselves: it is the gift of God.

EPHESIANS 2:8

If any of you lack wisdom, let him ask of God, that giveth to all men liberally, and upbraideth not; and it shall be given him.

But let him ask in faith, nothing wavering. For he that wavereth is like a wave of the sea driven with the wind and tossed.

JAMES 1:5–6

As ye have therefore received Christ Jesus the Lord, so walk ye in him:

Rooted and built up in him, and stablished in the faith, as ye have been taught, abounding therein with thanksgiving.

COLOSSIANS 2:6–7

For ye are all the children of God by faith in Christ Jesus.

GALATIANS 3:26

The fruit of the Spirit is love, joy, peace, longsuffering,

gentleness, goodness, faith,

Meekness, temperance: against such there is no law.

GALATIANS 5:22–23

And Jesus answering saith unto them, Have faith in God.

For verily I say unto you, That whosoever shall say unto this mountain, Be thou removed, and be thou cast into the sea; and shall not doubt in his heart, but shall believe that those things which he saith shall come to pass; he shall have whatsoever he saith.

MARK 11:22–23

You can keep a faith only as you can keep a plant, by rooting it into your life and making it grow there.
—PHILLIPS BROOKS

For we walk by faith, not by sight.

2 CORINTHIANS 5:7

But continue thou in the things which thou hast learned and hast been assured of, knowing of whom thou hast learned them;

And that from a child thou hast known the holy scriptures, which are able to make thee wise unto salvation through faith which is in Christ Jesus.

2 TIMOTHY 3:14–15

He that cometh to God must believe that he is, and that he is a rewarder of them that diligently seek him.

HEBREWS 11:6

That Christ may dwell in your hearts by faith; that ye, being rooted and grounded in love,

May be able to comprehend with all saints what is the breadth, and length, and depth, and height;

And to know the love of Christ, which passeth knowledge, that ye might be filled with all the fulness of God.

EPHESIANS 3:17–19

Wherefore seeing we also are compassed about with so great a cloud of witnesses, let us lay aside every weight, and the sin which doth so easily beset us, and let us run with patience the race that is set before us,

Looking unto Jesus the author and finisher of our faith; who for the joy that was set before him endured the cross, despising the shame, and is set down at the right hand of the throne of God.

HEBREWS 12:1–2

And Jesus said unto them, Because of your unbelief: for verily I say unto you, If ye have faith as a grain of mustard seed, ye shall say unto this mountain, Remove hence to yonder place; and it shall remove; and nothing shall be impossible unto you.

MATTHEW 17:20

For therein is the righteousness of God revealed from faith to faith: as it is written, The just shall live by faith.

ROMANS 1:17

Knowing that a man is not justified by the works of the law, but by the faith of Jesus Christ, even we have believed in Jesus Christ, that we might be justified by the faith of Christ, and not by the works of the law: for by the works of the law shall no flesh be justified.

GALATIANS 2:16

Faith means being grasped by a power that is greater than we are, a power that shakes us and turns us, and transforms and heals us. Surrender to this power of faith.

—PAUL TILLICH

Above all, taking the shield of faith, wherewith ye shall be able to quench all the fiery darts of the wicked.

EPHESIANS 6:16

Faithfulness, God's

Father, I am so glad that Your faithfulness is complete and eternal. Help me to always rely on You, rather than on human beings or the material world. I know You will never fail me. Amen.

He hath remembered his covenant for ever, the word which he commanded to a thousand generations.

PSALM 105:8

Let us hold fast the profession of our faith without wavering; (for he is faithful that promised).

HEBREWS 10:23

I can be calm and free from care
On any shore, since God is there.
—MADAME JEANNE GUYON

Know therefore that the LORD thy God, he is God, the faithful God, which keepeth covenant and mercy with them that love him and keep his commandments to a thousand generations.

DEUTERONOMY 7:9

(For thy LORD thy God is a merciful God;) he will not forsake thee, neither destroy thee, nor forget the covenant of thy fathers which he sware unto them.

DEUTERONOMY 4:31

Blessed be the LORD, that hath given rest unto his people Israel, according to all that he promised: there hath not failed one word of all his good promise.

1 KINGS 8:56

God is not a man, that he should lie; neither the son of man, that he should repent: hath he said, and shall he not do it? or hath he spoken, and shall he not make it good?

NUMBERS 23:19

If we believe not, yet he abideth faithful: he cannot deny himself.

2 TIMOTHY 2:13

The Lord is not slack concerning his promise, as some men count slackness; but is longsuffering to us-ward.

2 PETER 3:9

And they that know thy name will put their trust in thee: for thou, LORD, hast not forsaken them that seek thee.

PSALM 9:10

My covenant will I not break, nor alter the thing that is gone out of my lips.

PSALM 89:34

O LORD, thou art my God; I will exalt thee, I will praise thy name; for thou hast done wonderful things; thy counsels of old are faithfulness and truth.

ISAIAH 25:1

Thy word is true from the beginnand every one of thy righteous judgments endureth for ever.

PSALM 119:160

For ever, O LORD, thy word is settled in heaven.
Thy faithfulness is unto all generations.

PSALM 119:89–90

And also the Strength of Israel will not lie nor repent: for he is not a man, that he should repent.

1 SAMUEL 15:29

God is always with us;
why should we not always be with God?
—W. B. ULLATHORNE

For the mountains shall depart, and the hills be removed; but my kindness shall not depart from thee, neither shall the covenant of my peace be removed, saith the LORD that hath mercy on thee.

ISAIAH 54:10

Fear

*Jesus, You know how scared I am sometimes, even when I
hide it from those around me. Please take my fears, Lord.
Sometimes they're all I have to give You. They don't seem
like much of an offering—but here they are, Jesus.
I'm putting them in Your hands. Amen.*

And he said unto them, Why are ye so fearful? how is it that ye have no faith?

Mark 4:40

Fear not, little flock; for it is your Father's good pleasure to give you the kingdom.

Luke 12:32

Be still, my soul! thy God doth undertake
To guide thy future as he has the past.
Thy hope, thy confidence let nothing shake;
All now mysterious shall be bright at last.
Be still, my soul! the waves and winds still
knowHis voice who ruled them while
he dwelt below.
—Katharina A. von Schlegel

For I the Lord thy God will hold thy right hand, saying unto thee, Fear not; I will help thee.

Isaiah 41:13

But whoso hearkeneth unto me shall dwell safely, and shall be quiet from fear of evil.

Proverbs 1:33

For God hath not given us the spirit of fear; but of power, and of love, and of a sound mind.

2 Timothy 1:7

And fear not them which kill the body, but are not able to kill the soul.

Matthew 10:28

Be not afraid of sudden fear, neither of the desolation of the wicked, when it cometh.

For the Lord shall be thy confidence, and shall keep thy foot from being taken.

Proverbs 3:25–26

For ye have not received the spirit of bondage again to fear; but ye have received the Spirit of adoption, whereby we cry, Abba, Father.

Romans 8:15

The fear of man bringeth a snare: but whoso putteth his trust in the Lord shall be safe.

Proverbs 29:25

And it shall come to pass in the day that the Lord shall give thee rest from thy sorrow, and from thy fear, and from the hard bondage wherein thou wast made to serve.

Isaiah 14:3

When thou liest down, thou shalt not be afraid: yea, thou shalt lie down, and thy sleep shall be sweet.

Proverbs 3:24

God is our refuge and strength, a very present help in trouble.

PSALM 46:1

For the eyes of the Lord are over the righteous, and his ears are open unto their prayers: but the face of the Lord is against them that do evil.

And who is he that will harm you, if ye be followers of that which is good?

But and if ye suffer for righteousness' sake, happy are ye: and be not afraid of their terror, neither be troubled.

1 PETER 3:12–14

Peace I leave with you, my peace I give unto you: not as the world giveth, give I unto you. Let not your heart be troubled, neither let it be afraid.

JOHN 14:27

He shall cover thee with his feathers, and under his wings shalt thou trust: his truth shall be thy shield and buckler.

Thou shalt not be afraid for the terror by night; nor for the arrow that flieth by day;

Nor for the pestilence that walketh in darkness; nor for the destruction that wasteth at noonday.

PSALM 91:4–6

When thou passest through the waters, I will be with thee; and through the rivers, they shall not overflow thee: when thou walkest through the fire, thou shalt not be burned; neither shall the flame kindle upon thee.

ISAIAH 43:2

In righteousness shalt thou be established: thou shalt be far from oppression; for thou shalt not fear: and from terror; for it shall not come near thee.

ISAIAH 54:14

So that we may boldly say, The Lord is my helper, and I will not fear what man shall do unto me.

HEBREWS 13:6

Fear knocked at the door.
Faith answered. No one was there.
—INSCRIPTION ON AN ANCIENT MANTELPIECE
IN HIND'S HEAD HOTEL, BRAY, ENGLAND

I, even I, am he that comforteth you: who art thou, that thou shouldest be afraid of a man that shall die, and of the son of man which shall be made as grass.

ISAIAH 51:12

Fear not; for thou shalt not be ashamed: neither be thou confounded; for thou shalt not be put to shame: for thou shalt forget the shame of thy youth, and shalt not remember the reproach of thy widowhood any more.

ISAIAH 54:4

Food and
Clothing

*Food and clothing can seem so important sometimes, God.
Remind me, though, not to obsess about these things, but
to trust them to You. You know what I need, and You've
promised to care for me. I'm relying on You. Amen.*

And ye shall eat in plenty, and be satisfied, and praise the name of the LORD your God, that hath dealt wondrously with you: and my people shall never be ashamed.

JOEL 2:26

He maketh peace in thy borders, and filleth thee with the finest of the wheat.

PSALM 147:14

He hath given meat unto them that fear him: he will ever be mindful of his covenant.

PSALM 111:5

The righteous eateth to the satisfying of his soul: but the belly of the wicked shall want.

PROVERBS 13:25

I will abundantly bless her provision: I will satisfy her poor with bread.

PSALM 132:15

The people asked, and he brought quails, and satisfied them with the bread of heaven.

PSALM 105:40

Therefore take no thought, saying, What shall we eat? or, What shall we drink? or, Wherewithal shall we be clothed?

(For after all these things do the Gentiles seek:) for your heavenly Father knoweth that ye have need of all these things.

MATTHEW 6:31–32

We ought to repose on
Divine Providence,
not only for what concerns
temporal things, but much more
for what relates to our
spiritual life and perfection.
—Francis de Sales

Give us this day our daily bread.

Matthew 6:11

Forgiveness

When I'm having a hard time
forgiving someone, Lord, remind me of
how many times You've forgiven me. Amen.

Therefore if thine enemy hunger, feed him; if he thirst, give him drink.

ROMANS 12:20

"I can forgive, but I cannot forget," is only another way of saying, "I will not forgive."
A forgiveness ought to be like a cancelled note, torn in two and burned up, so that it can never be shown against the man.
—HENRY WARD BEECHER

But I say unto you, Love your enemies, bless them that curse you, do good to them that hate you, and pray for them which despitefully use you, and persecute you;

That ye may be the children of your Father which is in heaven: for he maketh his sun to rise on the evil and on the good, and sendeth rain on the just and on the unjust.

MATTHEW 5:44–45

For if ye forgive men their trespasses, your heavenly Father will also forgive you.

MATTHEW 6:14

But love ye your enemies, and do good, and lend, hoping for nothing again; and your reward shall be great, and ye shall be the children of the Highest: for he is kind unto the unthankful and to the evil.

Be ye therefore merciful, as your Father also is merciful.

Judge not, and ye shall not be judged: condemn not, and ye shall not be condemned: forgive, and ye shall be forgiven.

LUKE 6:35–37

And when ye stand praying, forgive, if ye have ought against any: that your Father also which is in heaven may forgive you your trespasses.

But if ye do not forgive, neither will your Father which is in heaven forgive your trespasses.

MARK 11:25–26

Say not thou, I will recompense evil; but wait on the LORD, and he shall save thee.

PROVERBS 20:22

Then came Peter to him, and said, Lord, how oft shall my brother sin against me, and I forgive him? till seven times? Jesus saith unto him, I say not unto thee, Until seven times: but, Until seventy times seven.

Therefore is the kingdom of heaven likened unto a certain king, which would take account of his servants.

MATTHEW 18:21–23

Take heed to yourselves: If thy brother trespass against thee, rebuke him; and if he repent, forgive him.

LUKE 17:3

Then said Jesus, Father, forgive them; for they know not what they do. And they parted his raiment, and cast lots.

LUKE 23:34

So that contrariwise ye ought rather to forgive him, and comfort him, lest perhaps such a one should be swallowed up with overmuch sorrow.

Wherefore I beseech you that ye would confirm your love toward him.

To whom ye forgive any thing, I forgive also: for if I forgave any thing, to whom I forgave it, for your sakes forgave I it in the person of Christ.

2 CORINTHIANS 2:7–8, 10

And forgive us our sins; for we also forgive every one that is indebted to us. And lead us not into temptation; but deliver us from evil.

LUKE 11:4

If we confess our sins, he is faithful and just to forgive us our sins, and to cleanse us from all unrighteousness.

1 JOHN 1:9

In whom we have redemption through his blood, the forgiveness of sins, according to the riches of his grace.

EPHESIANS 1:7

And be ye kind one to another, tenderhearted, forgiving one another, even as God for Christ's sake hath forgiven you.

EPHESIANS 4:32

Where is the foolish person who would
think it in his power to commit more
than God could forgive?
—FRANCIS DE SALES

And you, being dead in your sins and the uncircumcision of your flesh, hath he quickened together with him, having forgiven you all trespasses;

Blotting out the handwriting of ordinances that was against us, which was contrary to us, and took it out of the way, nailing it to his cross.

COLOSSIANS 2:13–14

In whom we have redemption through his blood, even the forgiveness of sins.

COLOSSIANS 1:14

Grace

*Thank You, Jesus, for the amazing
reality of Your grace. Amen.*

For the LORD God is a sun and shield: the LORD will give grace and glory: no good thing will he withhold from them that walk uprightly.

PSALM 84:11

Surely he scorneth the scorners: but he giveth grace unto the lowly.

PROVERBS 3:34

And now, brethren, I commend you to God, and to the word of his grace, which is able to build you up, and to give you an inheritance among all them which are sanctified.

ACTS 20:32

For the law was given by Moses, but grace and truth came by Jesus Christ.

JOHN 1:17

By whom also we have access by faith into this grace wherein we stand, and rejoice in hope of the glory of God.

ROMANS 5:2

For the grace of God that bringeth salvation hath appeared to all men.

TITUS 2:11

For our rejoicing is this, the testimony of our conscience, that in simplicity and godly sincerity, not with fleshly wisdom, but by the grace of God, we have had our conversation in the world, and more abundantly to you-ward.

2 CORINTHIANS 1:12

But not as the offence, so also is the free gift. For if through the offence of one many be dead, much more the grace of God, and the gift by grace, which is by one man, Jesus Christ, hath abounded unto many.

For if by one man's offence death reigned by one; much more they which receive abundance of grace and of the gift of righteousness shall reign in life by one, Jesus Christ.

That as sin hath reigned unto death, even so might grace reign through righteousness unto eternal life by Jesus Christ our Lord.

ROMANS 5:15, 17, 21

The grace of God is found in His great love for sinners, in His longing to do them good. His Son Jesus Christ personifies grace, for by the offering up of His body, sinners are made whole and pure, once and for all.
—JOHN BUNYAN

For by grace are ye saved through faith; and that not of yourselves: it is the gift of God.

EPHESIANS 2:8

What shall we say then? Shall we continue in sin, that grace may abound?

ROMANS 6:11

For sin shall not have dominion over you: for ye are not under the law, but under grace.

What then? shall we sin, because we are not under the law, but under grace? God forbid.

ROMANS 6:1, 14–15

For all things are for your sakes, that the abundant grace might through the thanksgiving of many redound to the glory of God.

2 CORINTHIANS 4:15

And he said unto me, My grace is sufficient for thee: for my strength is made perfect in weakness. Most gladly therefore will I rather glory in my infirmities, that the power of Christ may rest upon me.

2 CORINTHIANS 12:9

Guidance

Direct my life's paths, Lord.
I want to follow You. Please show me
the way. Amen.

And thine ears shall hear a word behind thee, saying, This is the way, walk ye in it, when ye turn to the right hand, and when ye turn to the left.

ISAIAH 30:21

For this God is our God for ever and ever: he will be our guide even unto death.

PSALM 48:14

A man's heart deviseth his way: but the LORD directeth his steps.

PROVERBS 16:9

Go Godward; thou wilt find a road.
—RUSSIAN PROVERB

The steps of a good man are ordered by the LORD: and he delighteth in his way.

PSALM 37:23

The righteousness of the perfect shall direct his way: but the wicked shall fall by his own wickedness.

PROVERBS 11:5

For his God doth instruct him to discretion, and doth teach him.

ISAIAH 28:26

And I will bring the blind by a way that they knew not; I will lead them in paths that they have not known: I will make darkness light before them, and crooked things straight. These things will I do unto them, and not forsake them.

ISAIAH 42:16

In all thy ways acknowledge him, and he shall direct thy paths.

PROVERBS 3:6

Nevertheless I am continually with thee: thou hast holden me by my right hand.

Thou shalt guide me with thy counsel, and afterward receive me to glory.

PSALM 73:23–24

For thou art my rock and my fortress; therefore for thy name's sake lead me, and guide me.

PSALM 31:3

Lead me, O LORD, in thy righteousness because of mine enemies; make thy way straight before my face.

PSALM 5:8

Lead me in thy truth, and teach me: for thou art the God of my salvation; on thee do I wait all the day.

PSALM 25:5

O send out thy light and thy truth: let them lead me; let them bring me unto thy holy hill, and to thy tabernacles.

PSALM 43:3

But made his own people to go forth like sheep, and guided them in the wilderness like a flock.

And he led them on safely, so that they feared not: but the sea overwhelmed their enemies.

And he brought them to the border of his sanctuary, even to this mountain, which his right hand had purchased.

PSALM 78:52–54

We plan—and God steps in with another plan for us and he is all-wise and the most loving friend we have always helping us.
—NETTIE FOWLER McCORMICK

And the LORD shall guide thee continually, and satisfy thy soul in drought, and make fat thy bones: and thou shalt be like a watered garden, and like a spring of water, whose waters fail not.

ISAIAH 58:11

To give light to them that sit in darkness and in the shadow of death, to guide our feet into the way of peace.

LUKE 1:79

I lead in the way of righteousness, in the midst of the paths of judgment.

PROVERBS 8:20

Guilt

I am so grateful, Christ, that in Your eyes I am no longer guilty. Thank You for all You did to make me clean and whole. Amen.

If we confess our sins, he is faithful and just to forgive us our sins, and to cleanse us from all unrighteousness.

1 JOHN 1:9

Let the wicked forsake his way, and the unrighteous man his thoughts: and let him return unto the LORD, and he will have mercy upon him; and to our God, for he will abundantly pardon.

ISAIAH 55:7

I take my heart in my hand,
O my God, O my God,
My broken heart in my hand:
Thou hast seen, judge thou.
—CHRISTINA ROSSETTI

And I will cleanse them from all their iniquity, whereby they have sinned against me; and I will pardon all their iniquities, whereby they have sinned, and whereby they have transgressed against me.

JEREMIAH 33:8

As far as the east is from the west, so far hath he removed our transgressions from us.

PSALM 103:12

For the LORD your God is gracious and merciful, and will not turn away his face from you, if ye return unto him.

2 CHRONICLES 30:9

For if our heart condemn us, God is greater than our heart, and knoweth all things.

1 JOHN 3:20

For I will be merciful to their unrighteousness, and their sins and their iniquities will I remember no more.

HEBREWS 8:12

Therefore if any man be in Christ, he is a new creature: old things are passed away; behold, all things are become new.

2 CORINTHIANS 5:17

But if we walk in the light, as he is in the light, we have fellowship one with another, and the blood of Jesus Christ his Son cleanseth us from all sin.

1 JOHN 1:7

For I will forgive their iniquity, and I will remember their sin no more.

JEREMIAH 31:34

Help in Troubles

When troubles come, God,
help me to trust in You. Amen.

Behold, God will not cast away a perfect man, neither will he help the evil doers:

Till he fill thy mouth with laughing, and thy lips with rejoicing.

Job 8:20–21

Be still, my soul! the Lord is on thy side;
Bear patiently the cross of grief or pain;
Leave to thy God to order and provide;
In every change he faithful will remain.
Be still, my soul! thy best, thy heavenly Friend
Thro' thorny ways leads to a joyful end.
—Katharina A. von Schlegel

Rejoice not against me, O mine enemy: when I fall, I shall arise; when I sit in darkness, the Lord shall be a light unto me.

I will bear the indignation of the Lord, because I have sinned against him, until he plead my cause, and execute judgment for me: he will bring me forth to the light, and I shall behold his righteousness.

Micah 7:8–9

These things I have spoken unto you, that in me ye

might have peace. In the world ye shall have tribulation: but be of good cheer; I have overcome the world.

JOHN 16:33

The LORD is good, a strong hold in the day of trouble; and he knoweth them that trust in him.

NAHUM 1:7

Why art thou cast down, O my soul? and why art thou disquieted within me? hope thou in God: for I shall yet praise him, who is the health of my countenance, and my God.

PSALM 42:11

There shall no evil befall thee, neither shall any plague come nigh thy dwelling.

For he shall give his angels charge over thee, to keep thee in all thy ways.

PSALM 91:10–11

Thou art my hiding place; thou shalt preserve me from trouble; thou shalt compass me about with songs of deliverance.

PSALM 32:7

Many are the afflictions of the righteous: but the LORD delivereth him out of them all.

PSALM 34:19

Though he fall, he shall not be utterly cast down: for the LORD upholdeth him with his hand.

PSALM 37:24

But the salvation of the righteous is of the LORD: he is their strength in the time of trouble.

PSALM 37:39

Though ye have lien among the pots, yet shall ye be as the wings of a dove covered with silver, and her feathers with yellow gold.

PSALM 68:13

Thou, which hast shewed me great and sore troubles, shalt quicken me again, and shalt bring me up again from the depths of the earth.

PSALM 71:20

They that sow in tears shall reap in joy.

He that goeth forth and weepeth, bearing precious seed, shall doubtless come again with rejoicing, bringing his sheaves with him.

PSALM 126:5–6

The LORD openeth the eyes of the blind: the LORD raiseth them that are bowed down: the LORD loveth the righteous.

PSALM 146:8

My flesh and my heart faileth: but God is the strength of my heart, and my portion for ever.

PSALM 73:26

O love the LORD, all ye his saints: for the LORD preserveth the faithful, and plentifully rewardeth the proud doer.

PSALM 31:23

For he hath not despised nor abhorred the affliction of the afflicted; neither hath he hid his face from him; but when he cried unto him, he heard.

PSALM 22:24

The LORD also will be a refuge for the oppressed, a refuge in times of trouble.

PSALM 9:9

Suffering is a test of faith. . .
If God's love calls you in suffering, respond
by self-surrender, and you will learn
the mystery of love.
—J. MESSNER

He shall deliver thee in six troubles: yea, in seven there shall no evil touch thee.

JOB 5:19

Though I walk in the midst of trouble, thou wilt revive me: thou shalt stretch forth thine hand against the wrath of mine enemies, and thy right hand shall save me.

PSALM 138:7

Holy Spirit

*Holy Spirit, live in my life. May I look
for You everywhere—and may I
open myself to You completely. Amen.*

Behold, I will pour out my spirit unto you, I will make known my words unto you.

PROVERBS 1:23

Likewise the Spirit also helpeth our infirmities: for we know not what we should pray for as we ought: but the Spirit itself maketh intercession for us with groanings which cannot be uttered.

And he that searcheth the hearts knoweth what is the mind of the Spirit, because he maketh intercession for the saints according to the will of God.

ROMANS 8:26–27

He that believeth on me, as the scripture hath said, out of his belly shall flow rivers of living water.

(But this spake he of the Spirit, which they that believe on him should receive: for the Holy Ghost was not yet given; because that Jesus was not yet glorified.)

JOHN 7:38–39

If ye then, being evil, know how to give good gifts unto your children: how much more shall your heavenly Father give the Holy Spirit to them that ask him?

LUKE 11:13

And I will pray the Father, and he shall give you another Comforter, that he may abide with you for ever;

Even the Spirit of truth; whom the world cannot receive, because it seeth him not, neither knoweth him: but ye know him; for he dwelleth with you, and shall be in you.

JOHN 14:16–17

As for me, this is my convenant with them, saith the LORD; My spirit that is upon thee, and my words which I have put in thy mouth, shall not depart out of thy mouth, nor out of the mouth of thy seed, nor out of the mouth of thy seed's seed, saith the LORD, from henceforth and for ever.

ISAIAH 59:21

Just as transparent substances, when subjected to light, themselves glitter and give off light, so does the soul, illuminated by the Holy Spirit, give light to others and itself become spiritual.
—ST. BASIL

Howbeit when he, the Spirit of truth, is come, he will guide you into all truth: for he shall not speak of himself; but whatsoever he shall hear, that shall he speak: and he will shew you things to come.

JOHN 16:13

That the blessing of Abraham might come on the Gentiles through Jesus Christ; that we might receive the promise of the Spirit through faith.

GALATIANS 3:14

Honesty

Lord, I'm not always honest—not even with myself.
Reveal the small lies and secret dishonesties that I hide in
my life. Make me completely clean. Make me like You.
Amen.

Ye shall not steal, neither deal falsely, neither lie one to another.   LEVITICUS 19:11

That no man go beyond and defraud his brother in any matter: because that the Lord is the avenger of all such, as we also have forewarned you and testified.

For God hath not called us unto uncleanness, but unto holiness.

1 THESSALONIANS 4:6–7

$\mathcal{T}$o be really honest means. . .making confession whether you can afford it or not; refusing unmerited praise; looking painful truths in the face.

—AUBREY DE VERE

The wicked borroweth, and payeth not again: but the righteous sheweth mercy, and giveth.

PSALM 37:21

Lie not one to another, seeing that ye have put off the old man with his deeds;

And have put on the new man, which is renewed in knowledge after the image of him that created him.

COLOSSIANS 3:9–10

Are there yet the treasures of wickedness in the house of the wicked, and the scant measure that is abominable?

Shall I count them pure with the wicked balances, and with the bag of deceitful weights?

For the rich men thereof are full of violence, and the inhabitants thereof have spoken lies, and their tongue is deceitful in their mouth.

MICAH 6:10–12

Ye shall do no unrighteousness in judgment, in mete-yard, in weight, or in measure.

LEVITICUS 19:35

A false balance is abomination to the LORD: but a just weight is his delight.

PROVERBS 11:1

Ye shall not therefore oppress one another; but thou shalt fear thy God: for I am the LORD your God.

LEVITICUS 25:17

But thou shalt have a perfect and just weight, a perfect and just measure shalt thou have: that thy days may be lengthened in the land which the LORD thy God giveth thee.

For all that do such things, and all that do unrighteously, are an abomination unto the LORD thy God.

DEUTERONOMY 25:15–16

Better is a little with righteousness than great revenues without right.

PROVERBS 16:8

hope

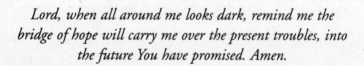

Lord, when all around me looks dark, remind me the bridge of hope will carry me over the present troubles, into the future You have promised. Amen.

Why art thou cast down, O my soul? and why art thou disquieted within me? hope thou in God: for I shall yet praise him, who is the health of my countenance, and my God.

PSALM 42:11

Which is Christ in you, the hope of glory.

COLOSSIANS 1:27

Be of good courage, and he shall strengthen your heart, all ye that hope in the LORD.

PSALM 31:24

For thou art my hope, O Lord GOD: thou art my trust from my youth.

PSALM 71:5

Who by him do believe in God, that raised him up from the dead, and gave him glory; that your faith and hope might be in God.

1 PETER 1:21

For the hope which is laid up for you in heaven, whereof ye heard before in the word of the truth of the gospel.

COLOSSIANS 1:5

Blessed be the God and Father of our Lord Jesus Christ, which according to his abundant mercy hath begotten us again unto a lively hope by the resurrection of Jesus Christ from the dead.

1 PETER 1:3

Wherefore gird up the loins of your mind, be sober, and hope to the end for the grace that is to be brought unto you at the revelation of Jesus Christ.

1 PETER 1:13

And every man that hath this hope in him purifieth himself, even as he is pure.

1 JOHN 3:3

Hope is the thing with feathers
That perches in the soul
And sings the tune without the words,
And never stops at all
And sweetest in the gale is heard.
—EMILY DICKINSON

If thou prepare thine heart, and stretch out thine hands toward him.

JOB 11:13

Happy is he that hath the God of Jacob for his help, whose hope is in the LORD his God.

PSALM 146:5

Blessed is the man that trusteth in the LORD, and whose hope the LORD is.

For he shall be as a tree planted by the waters, and that spreadeth out her roots by the river, and shall not see when heat cometh, but her leaf shall be green; and shall not be careful in the year of drought, neither shall cease from yielding fruit.

JEREMIAH 17:7–8

Now the God of hope fill you with all joy and peace in believing, that ye may abound in hope, through the power of the Holy Ghost.

ROMANS 15:13

Not boasting of things without our measure, that is, of other men's labours; but having hope, when your faith is increased, that we shall be enlarged by you according to our rule abundantly.

2 CORINTHIANS 10:15

Looking for that blessed hope, and the glorious appearing of the great God and our Saviour Jesus Christ.

TITUS 2:13

And not only so, but we glory in tribulations also: knowing that tribulation worketh patience;

And patience, experience; and experience, hope:

And hope maketh not ashamed; because the love of God is shed abroad in our hearts by the Holy Ghost which is given unto us.

ROMANS 5:3–5

Therefore my heart is glad, and my glory rejoiceth: my flesh also shall rest in hope.

PSALM 16:9

For in thee, O LORD, do I hope: thou wilt hear, O LORD my God.

PSALM 38:15

And now, Lord, what wait I for? my hope is in thee.

PSALM 39:7

The future is full of doubt, indeed, but fuller still of hope.
—JOHN LUBBOCK

Why art thou cast down, O my soul? and why art thou disquieted in me? hope thou in God: for I shall yet praise him for the help of his countenance.

PSALM 42:5

Thou art my hiding place and my shield: I hope in thy word.

Uphold me according unto thy word, that I may live: and let me not be ashamed of my hope.

PSALM 119:114, 116

Hospitality

*Father, may my home be a place where others
feel welcomed and loved. Most of all, God,
may my home be always open to You. Please
live here with me. Amen.*

Be not forgetful to entertain strangers: for thereby some have entertained angels unawares.

HEBREWS 13:2

For whosoever shall give you a cup of water to drink in my name, because ye belong to Christ, verily I say unto you, he shall not lose his reward.

MARK 9:41

While the spirit of neighborliness was important on the frontier because neighbors were so few, it is even more important now because our neighbors are so many.
—CLAUDIA "LADY BIRD" JOHNSON

Use hospitality one to another without grudging.

As every man hath received the gift, even so minister the same one to another, as good stewards of the manifold grace of God.

1 PETER 4:9–10

If a brother or sister be naked, and destitute of daily food,

And one of you say unto them, Depart in peace, be ye warmed and filled; notwithstanding ye give them not those things which are needful to the body; what doth it profit?

JAMES 2:15–16

I have shewed you all things, how that so labouring ye ought to support the weak, and to remember the words of the Lord Jesus, how he said, It is more blessed to give than to receive.

ACTS 20:35

But whoso hath this world's good, and seeth his brother have need, and shutteth up his bowels of compassion from him, how dwelleth the love of God in him?

1 JOHN 3:17

Distributing to the necessity of saints; given to hospitality.

ROMANS 12:13

For I was an hungered, and ye gave me meat: I was thirsty, and ye gave me drink: I was a stranger, and ye took me in:

Naked, and ye clothed me: I was sick, and ye visited me: I was in prison, and ye came unto me.

And the King shall answer and say unto them, Verily I say unto you, Inasmuch as ye have done it unto one of the least of these my brethren, ye have done it unto me.

MATTHEW 25:35–36, 40

humility

Trying to make myself feel humble, Lord, is a little like
trying to pull myself up by my own shoelaces.
I can't do it, God. So, please, You do it for me.
Fill my heart with humility. Amen.

Whosoever therefore shall humble himself as this little child, the same is greatest in the kingdom of heaven.

MATTHEW 18:4

LORD, thou hast heard the desire of the humble: thou wilt prepare their heart, thou wilt cause thine ear to hear.

PSALM 10:17

And whosoever shall exalt himself shall be abased; and he that shall humble himself shall be exalted.

MATTHEW 23:12

When men are cast down, then thou shalt say, There is lifting up; and he shall save the humble person.

JOB 22:29

Better it is to be of an humble spirit with the lowly, than to divide the spoil with the proud.

PROVERBS 16:19

Surely he scorneth the scorners: but he giveth grace unto the lowly.

PROVERBS 3:34

But he giveth more grace. Wherefore he saith, God resisteth the proud, but giveth grace unto the humble.

JAMES 4:6

When he maketh inquisition for blood, he remembereth them: he forgetteth not the cry of the humble.

PSALM 9:12

By humility and the fear of the LORD are riches, and honour, and life.

PROVERBS 22:4

The fear of the LORD is the instruction of wisdom; and before honour is humility.

PROVERBS 15:33

humility like darkness
reveals the heavenly lights.
—HENRY DAVID THOREAU

A man's pride shall bring him low: but honour shall uphold the humble in spirit.

PROVERBS 29:23

Jealousy

Help me not to feel jealous, Lord, of those around me.
Remind me that You have given me everything I need.
I am complete in You, so why should I be
jealous of others? Amen.

For where envying and strife is, there is confusion and every evil work.

JAMES 3:16

Do ye think that the scripture saith in vain, The spirit that dwelleth in us lusteth to envy?

JAMES 4:5

A jealous person is doubly unhappy—over what he has, which is judged inferior, and over what he has not, which is judged superior. Such a person is doubly removed from knowing the true blessings of creation.

—DESMOND TUTU

Let us not be desirous of vain glory, provoking one another, envying one another.

GALATIANS 5:26

Neither shalt thou desire thy neighbour's wife, neither shalt thou covet thy neighbour's house, his field, or his manservant, or his maidservant, his ox, or his ass, or any thing that is thy neighbour's.

DEUTERONOMY 5:21

For the wicked boasteth of his heart's desire, and blesseth the covetous, whom the LORD abhorreth.

PSALM 10:3

Envy thou not the oppressor, and choose none of his ways.

PROVERBS 3:31

A sound heart is the life of the flesh: but envy the rottenness of the bones.

PROVERBS 14:30

Wrath is cruel, and anger is outrageous; but who is able to stand before envy?

PROVERBS 27:4

Let no man seek his own, but every man another's wealth.

1 CORINTHIANS 10:24

Rest in the LORD, and wait patiently for him: fret not thyself because of him who prospereth in his way, because of the man who bringeth wicked devices to pass.

PSALM 37:7

Again, I considered all travail, and every right work, that for this a man is envied of his neighbour. This is also vanity and vexation of spirit.

ECCLESIASTES 4:4

But if ye have bitter envying and strife in your hearts, glory not, and lie not against the truth.

JAMES 3:14

Joy

Remind me, God, to open myself to Your happiness
each day, each moment. Help me not to let life's
pressures and frustrations cloud my vision
of Your unending joy. Amen.

For ye shall go out with joy, and be led forth with peace: the mountains and the hills shall break forth before you into singing, and all the trees of the field shall clap their hands.

ISAIAH 55:12

They that sow in tears shall reap in joy.

He that goeth forth and weepeth, bearing precious seed, shall doubtless come again with rejoicing, bringing his sheaves with him.

PSALM 126:5–6

Blessed is the people that know the joyful sound: they shall walk, O LORD, in the light of thy countenance.

In thy name shall they rejoice all the day: and in thy righ-teousness shall they be exalted.

PSALM 89:15–16

The voice of rejoicing and salvation is in the tabernacles of the righteous: the right hand of the LORD doeth valiantly.

PSALM 118:15

Thou hast put gladness in my heart, more than in the time that their corn and their wine increased.

PSALM 4:7

These things I have spoken unto you, that my joy might remain in you, and that your joy might be full.

JOHN 15:11

Light is sown for the righteous, and gladness for the

upright in heart.

Rejoice in the LORD, ye righteous; and give thanks at the remembrance of his holiness.

PSALM 97:11–12

God cannot endure that unfestive, mirthless attitude of ours in which we eat our bread in sorrow, with pretentious, busy haste, or even with shame. Through our daily meals He is calling us to rejoice, to keep holiday in the midst of our working day.
—DIETRICH BONHOEFFER

For then shalt thou have thy delight in the Almighty, and shalt lift up thy face unto God.

JOB 22:26

Whom having not seen, ye love; in whom, though now ye see him not, yet believing, ye rejoice with joy unspeakable and full of glory.

1 PETER 1:8

Therefore the redeemed of the LORD shall return, and come with singing unto Zion; and everlasting joy shall be upon their head: they shall obtain gladness and joy; and sorrow and mourning shall flee away.

ISAIAH 51:11

For our heart shall rejoice in him, because we have trusted in his holy name.

PSALM 33:21

I will greatly rejoice in the LORD, my soul shall be joyful in my God; for he hath clothed me with the garments of salvation, he hath covered me with the robe of righteousness, as a bridegroom decketh himself with ornaments, and as a bride adorneth herself with her jewels.

ISAIAH 61:10

Then he said unto them, Go your way, eat the fat, and drink the sweet, and send portions unto them for whom nothing is prepared: for this day is holy unto our Lord: neither be ye sorry; for the joy of the LORD is your strength.

NEHEMIAH 8:10

Thou shalt fan them, and the wind shall carry them away, and the whirlwind shall scatter them: and thou shalt rejoice in the LORD, and shalt glory in the Holy One of Israel.

ISAIAH 41:16

The righteous shall be glad in the LORD, and shall trust in him; and all the upright in heart shall glory.

PSALM 64:10

My soul shall be satisfied as with marrow and fatness; and my mouth shall praise thee with joyful lips.

PSALM 63:5

But let the righteous be glad; let them rejoice before God: yea, let them exceedingly rejoice.

PSALM 68:3

And ye now therefore have sorrow: but I will see you again, and your heart shall rejoice, and your joy no man taketh from you.

JOHN 16:22

Cana of Galilee. . . Ah, that sweet miracle! It was not men's grief, but their joy Christ visited. He worked his first miracle to help men's gladness.
—FYODOR DOSTOEVSKY

And not only so, but we also joy in God through our Lord Jesus Christ, by whom we have now received the atonement.

ROMANS 5:11

Thou hast turned for me my mourning into dancing: thou hast put off my sackcloth, and girded me with gladness.

PSALM 30:11

Laziness

Jesus, thank You that my work is a gift to me
from You. Help me to find You in it. Amen.

He becometh poor that dealeth with a slack hand: but the hand of the diligent maketh rich.

He that gathereth in summer is a wise son: but he that sleepeth in harvest is a son that causeth shame.

PROVERBS 10:4–5

Not slothful in business; fervent in spirit; serving the Lord.

ROMANS 12:11

Where our work is, there let our joy be.
—TERTULLIAN

The soul of the sluggard desireth, and hath nothing: but the soul of the diligent shall be made fat.

PROVERBS 13:4

The husbandman that laboureth must be first partaker of the fruits.

2 TIMOTHY 2:6

Much food is in the tillage of the poor: but there is that is destroyed for want of judgment.

PROVERBS 13:23

For even when we were with you, this we commanded

you, that if any would not work, neither should he eat.

For we hear that there are some which walk among you disorderly, working not at all, but are busybodies.

Now them that are such we command and exhort by our Lord Jesus Christ, that with quietness they work, and eat their own bread.

2 THESSALONIANS 3:10–12

And that ye study to be quiet, and to do your own business, and to work with your own hands, as we commanded you;

That ye may walk honestly toward them that are without, and that ye may have lack of nothing.

1 THESSALONIANS 4:11–12

I went by the field of the slothful, and by the vineyard of the man void of understanding;

And, lo, it was all grown over with thorns, and nettles had covered the face thereof, and the stone wall thereof was broken down.

Then I saw, and considered it well: I looked upon it, and received instruction.

Yet a little sleep, a little slumber, a little folding of the hands to sleep:

So shall thy poverty come as one that travelleth; and thy want as an armed man.

PROVERBS 24:30–34

He that tilleth his land shall have plenty of bread: but he that followeth after vain persons shall have poverty enough.

PROVERBS 28:19

Love not sleep, lest thou come to poverty; open thine eyes, and thou shalt be satisfied with bread.

PROVERBS 20:13

The way of the slothful man is as an hedge of thorns: but the way of the righteous is made plain.

PROVERBS 15:19

Be thou diligent to know the state of thy flocks, and look well to thy herds.

PROVERBS 27:23

Let him that stole steal no more: but rather let him labour, working with his hands the thing which is good, that he may have to give to him that needeth.

EPHESIANS 4:28

The thoughts of the diligent tend only to plenteousness; but of every one that is hasty only to want.

PROVERBS 21:5

The hand of the diligent shall bear rule: but the slothful shall be under tribute.

PROVERBS 12:24

He that tilleth his land shall be satisfied with bread: but he that followeth vain persons is void of understanding.

PROVERBS 12:11

And thou shalt have goats' milk enough for thy food, for the food of thy household, and for the maintenance for thy maidens.

PROVERBS 27:27

Loneliness

I feel so lonely sometimes, God.
Thank You that even when I have no one else,
I always have Your Spirit's presence. Amen.

Then shalt thou call, and the LORD shall answer; thou shalt cry, and he shall say, Here I am.

ISAIAH 58:9

Since thou wast precious in my sight, thou hast been honourable, and I have loved thee.

ISAIAH 43:4

The soul hardly ever realizes it, but whether he is a believer or not, his loneliness is really a homesickness for God.
—HUBERT VAN ZELLER

And will be a Father unto you, and ye shall be my sons and daughters, saith the Lord Almighty.

2 CORINTHIANS 6:18

And, behold, I am with thee, and will keep thee in all places whither thou goest, and will bring thee again into this land; for I will not leave thee, until I have done that which I have spoken to thee of.

GENESIS 28:15

I will not leave you comfortless: I will come to you.

JOHN 14:18

And ye are complete in him, which is the head of all principality and power.

COLOSSIANS 2:10

But I am poor and needy; yet the Lord thinketh upon me: thou art my help and my deliverer; make no tarrying, O my God.

PSALM 40:17

Love,
Brotherly

*Thank You, Jesus, for all the people whom
I love. I know I see Your face in them—help
them to see You in me. Amen.*

A new commandment I give unto you, That ye love one another; as I have loved you, that ye also love one another.

By this shall all men know that ye are my disciples, if ye have love one to another.

JOHN 13:34–35

Seeing ye have purified your souls in obeying the truth through the Spirit unto unfeigned love of the brethren, see that ye love one another with a pure heart fervently.

I PETER 1:22

human love and the delights of friendship, out of which are built the memories that endure, are also to be treasured up as hints of what shall be hereafter.

—BEDE JARRETT

Let love be without dissimulation. Abhor that which is evil; cleave to that which is good.

Be kindly affectioned one to another with brotherly love; in honour preferring one another.

ROMANS 12:9–10

But as touching brotherly love ye need not that I write unto you: for ye yourselves are taught of God to love one another.

1 THESSALONIANS 4:9

He that loveth his brother abideth in the light, and there is none occasion of stumbling in him.

1 JOHN 2:10

Beloved, let us love one another: for love is of God; and every one that loveth is born of God, and knoweth God.

He that loveth not knoweth not God; for God is love.

1 JOHN 4:7–8

My little children, let us not love in word, neither in tongue; but in deed and in truth.

1 JOHN 3:18

Beloved, if God so loved us, we ought also to love one another.

1 JOHN 4:11

Put on therefore, as the elect of God, holy and beloved, bowels of mercies, kindness, humbleness of mind, meekness, longsuffering;

Forbearing one another, and forgiving one another, if any man have a quarrel against any: even as Christ forgave you, so also do ye.

COLOSSIANS 3:12–13

Love, God's

*I know, God, that Your love is beyond
my comprehension. Thank You that wherever I go,
whatever happens, I will never lose Your love. Amen.*

And we have known and believed the love that God hath to us. God is love; and he that dwelleth in love dwelleth in God, and God in him.

1 JOHN 4:16

For the Father himself loveth you, because ye have loved me, and have believed that I came out from God.

JOHN 16:27

We love him, because he first loved us.

1 JOHN 4:19

For God so loved the world, that he gave his only begotten Son, that whosoever believeth in him should not perish, but have everlasting life.

JOHN 3:16

The LORD openeth the eyes of the blind: the LORD raiseth them that are bowed down: the LORD loveth the righteous.

PSALM 146:8

The way of the wicked is an abomination unto the LORD: but he loveth him that followeth after righteousness.

PROVERBS 15:9

For as a young man marrieth a virgin, so shall thy sons marry thee: and as the bridegroom rejoiceth over the bride, so shall thy God rejoice over thee.

ISAIAH 62:5

Herein is love, not that we loved God, but that he loved

us, and sent his Son to be the propitiation for our sins.

1 JOHN 4:10

Yea, I will rejoice over them to do them good, and I will plant them in this land assuredly with my whole heart and with my whole soul.

JEREMIAH 32:41

I will heal their backsliding, I will love them freely: for mine anger is turned away from him.

HOSEA 14:4

Love is the greatest thing that God can give us; for He Himself is love; and it is the greatest thing we can give to God.
—JEREMY TAYLOR

The LORD thy God in the midst of thee is mighty; he will save, he will rejoice over thee with joy; he will rest in his love, he will joy over thee with singing.

ZEPHANIAH 3:17

And I have declared unto them thy name, and will declare it: that the love wherewith thou hast loved me may be in them, and I in them.

JOHN 17:26

And he will love thee, and bless thee, and multiply thee: he will also bless the fruit of thy womb, and the fruit of thy land, thy corn, and thy wine, and thine oil, the increase of thy kine, and the flocks of thy sheep, in the land which he sware unto thy fathers to give thee.

DEUTERONOMY 7:13

But God, who is rich in mercy, for his great love wherewith he loved us,

Even when we were dead in sins, hath quickened us together with Christ, (by grace ye are saved;)

And hath raised us up together, and made us sit together in heavenly places in Christ Jesus:

That in the ages to come he might shew the exceeding riches of his grace in his kindness toward us through Christ Jesus.

EPHESIANS 2:4–7

Now our Lord Jesus Christ himself, and God, even our Father, which hath loved us, and hath given us everlasting consolation and good hope through grace,

Comfort your hearts, and stablish you in every good word and work.

2 THESSALONIANS 2:16–17

Loving God

*Remind me, Jesus, that the best way to show You
my love is to show my love to the people around me.
Please help me to grow in love as I open myself more
and more to Your Spirit. Amen.*

Know therefore that the LORD thy God, he is God, the faithful God, which keepeth covenant and mercy with them that love him and keep his commandments to a thousand generations.

DEUTERONOMY 7:9

I love them that love me; and those that seek me early shall find me.

PROVERBS 8:17

Love of man leads to the love of God.
—INDIAN PROVERB

He that hath my commandments, and keepeth them, he it is that loveth me: and he that loveth me shall be loved of my Father, and I will love him, and will manifest myself to him.

JOHN 14:21

But as it is written, Eye hath not seen, nor ear heard, neither have entered into the heart of man, the things which God hath prepared for them that love him.

1 CORINTHIANS 2:9

That I may cause those that love me to inherit substance; and I will fill their treasures.

PROVERBS 8:21

Delight thyself also in the LORD; and he shall give thee the desires of thine heart.

PSALM 37:4

The LORD preserveth all them that love him: but all the wicked will he destroy.

PSALM 145:20

Because he hath set his love upon me, therefore will I deliver him: I will set him on high, because he hath known my name.

PSALM 91:14

Grace be with all them that love our Lord Jesus Christ in sincerity. Amen.

EPHESIANS 6:24

And it shall come to pass, if ye shall hearken diligently unto my commandments which I command you this day, to love the LORD your God, and to serve him with all your heart and with all your soul,

That I will give you the rain of your land in his due season, the first rain and the latter rain, that thou mayest gather in thy corn, and thy wine, and thine oil.

And I will send grass in thy fields for thy cattle, that thou mayest eat and be full.

DEUTERONOMY 11:13–15

Lust

*Lord, help me not to crave things that aren't healthy
for me, making them my god in Your place.
Be the Lord of my life. Amen.*

From whence come wars and fightings among you? come they not hence, even of your lusts that war in your members?

Ye lust, and have not: ye kill, and desire to have, and cannot obtain: ye fight and war, yet ye have not, because ye ask not.

Ye ask, and receive not, because ye ask amiss, that ye may consume it upon your lusts.

Ye adulterers and adulteresses, know ye not that the friendship of the world is enmity with God? whosoever therefore will be a friend of the world is the enemy of God.

JAMES 4:1–4

Whereby are given unto us exceeding great and precious promises: that by these ye might be partakers of the divine nature, having escaped the corruption that is in the world through lust.

2 PETER 1:4

For all that is in the world, the lust of the flesh, and the lust of the eyes, and the pride of life, is not of the Father, but is of the world.

And the world passeth away, and the lust thereof: but he that doeth the will of God abideth for ever.

1 JOHN 2:16–17

Ye have heard that it was said by them of old time, Thou shalt not commit adultery:

But I say unto you, That whosoever looketh on a woman to lust after her hath committed adultery with her already in his heart.

MATTHEW 5:27–28

As obedient children, not fashioning yourselves according to the former lusts in your ignorance:

But as he which hath called you is holy, so be ye holy in all manner of conversation;

Because it is written, Be ye holy; for I am holy.

1 PETER 1:14–16

Lust is an appetite by which temporal goods are preferred to eternal goods.
—ST. AUGUSTINE

Submit yourselves therefore to God. Resist the devil, and he will flee from you.

Draw nigh to God, and he will draw nigh to you. Cleanse your hands, ye sinners; and purify your hearts, ye double minded.

JAMES 4:7–8

For the grace of God that bringeth salvation hath appeared to all men,

Teaching us that, denying ungodliness and worldly lusts, we should live soberly, righteously, and godly, in this present world.

TITUS 2:11–12

Lying

Lord, make me a person of integrity. Amen.

Lie not one to another, seeing that ye have put off the old man with his deeds;

And have put on the new man, which is renewed in knowledge after the image of him that created him.

COLOSSIANS 3:9–10

And ye shall not swear by my name falsely, neither shalt thou profane the name of thy God: I am the LORD.

LEVITICUS 19:12

So long as we are able to distinguish any space whatever between the truth and us we remain outside it.
—HENRI AMIEL

How many times shall I adjure thee that thou tell me nothing but that which is true in the name of the LORD?

1 KINGS 22:16

The wicked are estranged from the womb: they go astray as soon as they be born, speaking lies.

PSALM 58:3

A faithful witness will not lie: but a false witness will utter lies.

PROVERBS 14:5

A false witness shall not be unpunished, and he that speaketh lies shall perish.

PROVERBS 19:9

A false witness shall not be unpunished, and he that speaketh lies shall not escape.

PROVERBS 19:5

Be not a witness against thy neighbour without cause; and deceive not with thy lips.

PROVERBS 24:28

If a false witness rise up against any man to testify against him that which is wrong;

Then both the men, between whom the controversy is, shall stand before the LORD, before the priests and the judges, which shall be in those days;

And the judges shall make diligent inquisition: and, behold, if the witness be a false witness, and hath testified falsely against his brother;

Then shall ye do unto him, as he had thought to have done unto his brother: so shalt thou put the evil away from among you.

DEUTERONOMY 19:16–19

A man that beareth false witness against his neighbour is a maul, and a sword, and a sharp arrow.

PROVERBS 25:18

Thou shalt not raise a false report: put not thine hand with the wicked to be an unrighteous witness.

Exodus 23:1

But if ye have bitter envying and strife in your hearts, glory not, and lie not against the truth.

James 3:14

The lip of truth shall be established for ever: but a lying tongue is but for a moment.

Proverbs 12:19

Whoever has even once become notorious
by base fraud, even if he speaks the truth,
gains no belief.
—Phaedrus

These six things doth the Lord hate: yea, seven are an abomination unto him:

A proud look, a lying tongue, and hands that shed innocent blood,

An heart that deviseth wicked imaginations, feet that be swift in running to mischief,

A false witness that speaketh lies, and he that soweth discord among brethren.

Proverbs 6:16–19

Marriage

God, I'm glad that You created the institution of marriage. Thank You for all the ways You reveal Yourself to the world through this special relationship. I pray Your blessing and strength and joy on all married people everywhere.
Amen.

Live joyfully with the wife whom thou lovest all the days of the life of thy vanity, which he hath given thee under the sun, all the days of thy vanity: for that is thy portion in this life, and in thy labour which thou takest under the sun.

ECCLESIASTES 9:9

Drink waters out of thine own cistern, and running waters out of thine own well.

PROVERBS 5:15

The goal in marriage is not to think alike, but to think together.
—ROBERT C. DODDS

Let the husband render unto the wife due benevolence: and likewise also the wife unto the husband.

1 CORINTHIANS 7:3

Wives, submit yourselves unto your own husbands, as unto the Lord.

For the husband is the head of the wife, even as Christ is the head of the church: and he is the saviour of the body.

EPHESIANS 5:22–23

Let thy fountain be blessed: and rejoice with the wife of thy youth.

Let her be as the loving hind and pleasant roe; let her breasts satisfy thee at all times; and be thou ravished always with her love.

And why wilt thou, my son, be ravished with a strange woman, and embrace the bosom of a stranger?

PROVERBS 5:18–20

Wives submit yourselves unto your own husbands, as it is fit in the Lord.

Husbands, love your wives, and be not bitter against them.

COLOSSIANS 3:18–19

Husbands, love your wives, even as Christ also loved the church, and gave himself for it.

EPHESIANS 5:25

So ought men to love their wives as their own bodies. He that loveth his wife loveth himself.

EPHESIANS 5:28

For this cause shall a man leave his father and mother, and shall be joined unto his wife, and they two shall be one flesh.

EPHESIANS 5:31

Mercy

*Thank You, God, for the mercy You showed us
when You sent Your Son to earth. I am so grateful
that Your mercy will never be used up,
that it will last forever. Amen.*

And therefore will the LORD wait, that he may be gracious unto you, and therefore will he be exalted, that he may have mercy upon you: for the LORD is a God of judgment: blessed are all they that wait for him.

ISAIAH 30:18

Know therefore that God exacteth of thee less than thine iniquity deserveth.

JOB 11:6

And I will have mercy upon her that had not obtained mercy; and I will say to them which were not my people, Thou art my people; and they shall say, Thou art my God.

HOSEA 2:23

He made known his ways unto Moses, his acts unto the children of Israel.

But the mercy of the LORD is from everlasting to everlasting upon them that fear him, and his righteousness unto children's children.

PSALM 103:7, 17

Like as a father pitieth his children, so the LORD pitieth them that fear him.

PSALM 103:13

And he said, I will make all my goodness pass before thee, and I will proclaim the name of the LORD before thee; and will be gracious to whom I will be gracious, and will shew mercy on whom I will shew mercy.

EXODUS 33:19

Who is a God like unto thee, that pardoneth iniquity, and passeth by the transgression of the remnant of his heritage? he retaineth not his anger for ever, because he delighteth in mercy.

MICAH 7:18

For in my wrath I smote thee, but in my favour have I had mercy on thee.

ISAIAH 60:10

Since God has mercies to give, and He intends to give them to us, those mercies are not broken pieces or someone else's leftovers. . . . God has bags that were never untied, never opened up, but set aside through a thousand generations for those who hope in His mercy.
—JOHN BUNYAN

For my name's sake will I defer mine anger, and for my praise will I refrain for thee, that I cut thee not off.

ISAIAH 48:9

The LORD will perfect that which concerneth me: thy mercy, O LORD, endureth for ever: forsake not the works of thine own hands.

PSALM 138:8

Behold, we count them happy which endure. Ye have heard of the patience of Job, and have seen the end of the Lord; that the Lord is very pitiful, and of tender mercy.

JAMES 5:11

And his mercy is on them that fear him from generation to generation.

LUKE 1:50

He is the tower of salvation for his king: and sheweth mercy to his anointed, unto David, and to his seed for evermore.

2 SAMUEL 22:51

Surely goodness and mercy shall follow me all the days of my life: and I will dwell in the house of the LORD for ever.

PSALM 23:6

All the paths of the LORD are mercy and truth unto such as keep his covenant and his testimonies.

PSALM 25:10

Many sorrows shall be to the wicked: but he that trusteth in the LORD, mercy shall compass him about.

PSALM 32:10

Withhold not thou thy tender mercies from me, O
LORD: let thy lovingkindness and thy truth continually
preserve me.

PSALM 40:11

His mercy hath no relation to time,
no limitation in time, it is not first, nor last,
but eternal, everlasting.
—JOHN DONNE

For he saith to Moses, I will have mercy on whom I will
have mercy, and I will have compassion on whom I will
have compassion.

So then it is not of him that willeth, nor of him that
runneth, but of God that sheweth mercy.

ROMANS 9:15–16

Money

Help me remember, God, that my money belongs to You. May I use it for Your glory. Keep me from making it the center of my life. Amen.

Labour not to be rich: cease from thine own wisdom.

Wilt thou set thine eyes upon that which is not? for riches certainly make themselves wings; they fly away as an eagle toward heaven.

PROVERBS 23:4–5

A little that a righteous man hath is better than the riches of many wicked.

PSALM 37:16

We ought to change the legend on our money from "In God We Trust" to "In Money We Trust." Because, as a nation, we've got far more faith in money these days than we do in God.
—ARTHUR HOPPE

Hearken, my beloved brethren, Hath not God chosen the poor of this world rich in faith, and heirs of the kingdom which he hath promised to them that love him?

JAMES 2:5

But he saveth the poor from the sword, from their mouth, and from the hand of the mighty.

So the poor hath hope, and iniquity stoppeth her mouth.

JOB 5:15–16

Better is an handful with quietness, than both the hands full with travail and vexation of spirit.

ECCLESIASTES 4:6

For the oppression of the poor, for the sighing of the needy, now will I arise, saith the LORD; I will set him in safety from him that puffeth at him.

PSALM 12:5

But thou shalt remember the LORD thy God: for it is he that giveth thee power to get wealth, that he may establish his covenant which he sware unto thy fathers, as it is this day.

DEUTERONOMY 8:18

Whoso mocketh the poor reproacheth his Maker: and he that is glad at calamities shall not be unpunished.

PROVERBS 17:5

Charge them that are rich in this world, that they be not highminded, nor trust in uncertain riches, but in the living God, who giveth us richly all things to enjoy;

That they do good, that they be rich in good works, ready to distribute, willing to communicate;

Laying up in store for themselves a good foundation against the time to come, that they may lay hold on eternal life.

I TIMOTHY 6:17–19

There is that maketh himself rich, yet hath nothing: there is that maketh himself poor, yet hath great riches.

PROVERBS 13:7

Rob not the poor, because he is poor: neither oppress the afflicted in the gate.

PROVERBS 22:22

The sleep of a labouring man is sweet, whether he eat little or much: but the abundance of the rich will not suffer him to sleep.

There is a sore evil which I have seen under the sun, namely, riches kept for the owners thereof to their hurt.

But those riches perish by evil travail: and he begetteth a son, and there is nothing in his hand.

ECCLESIASTES 5:12–14

He that loveth silver shall not be satisfied with silver; nor he that loveth abundance with increase: this is also vanity.

ECCLESIASTES 5:10

The rich and poor meet together: the LORD is the maker of them all.

PROVERBS 22:2

Better is little with the fear of the LORD than great treasure and trouble therewith.

PROVERBS 15:16

For the needy shall not alway be forgotten: the expectation of the poor shall not perish for ever.

PSALM 9:18

Obedience

Lord, give me the strength to be Your obedient child. May I say "yes" to whatever You send me. And remind me, Jesus, to be just as obedient with the small and trivial areas of my life as I am with the big and significant. Amen.

See, I have set before thee this day life and good, and death and evil;

In that I command thee this day to love the LORD thy God, to walk in his ways, and to keep his commandments and his statutes and his judgments, that thou mayest live and multiply: and the LORD thy God shall bless thee in the land whither thou goest to possess it.

DEUTERONOMY 30:15–16

He that strives to draw himself from obedience, withdraws himself from grace.
—THOMAS Á KEMPIS

And thou shalt do that which is right and good in the sight of the LORD: that it may be well with thee, and that thou mayest go in and possess the good land which the LORD sware unto thy fathers.

DEUTERONOMY 6:18

Hear therefore, O Israel, and observe to do it; that it may be well with thee, and that ye may increase mightily, as the LORD God of thy fathers hath promised thee, in the land that floweth with milk and honey.

DEUTERONOMY 6:3

Whosoever therefore shall break one of these least commandments, and shall teach men so, he shall be called
the least in the kingdom of heaven: but whosoever shall
do and teach them, the same shall be called great in the
kingdom of heaven.

MATTHEW 5:19

But whoso looketh into the perfect law of liberty, and
continueth therein, he being not a forgetful hearer, but a
doer of the work, this man shall be blessed in his deed.

JAMES 1:25

Wherefore it shall come to pass, if ye hearken to these
judgments, and keep, and do them, that the LORD thy
God shall keep unto thee the covenant and the mercy
which he sware unto thy fathers.

DEUTERONOMY 7:12

Keep therefore the words of this covenant, and do them,
that ye may prosper in all that ye do.

DEUTERONOMY 29:9

O that there were such an heart in them, that they would
fear me, and keep all my commandments always, that
it might be well with them, and with their children for
ever!

DEUTERONOMY 5:29

Those things, which ye have both learned, and received,
and heard, and seen in me, do: and the God of peace
shall be with you.

PHILIPPIANS 4:9

Verily, verily, I say unto you, He that heareth my word, and believeth on him that sent me, hath everlasting life, and shall not come into condemnation; but is passed from death unto life.

JOHN 5:24

Therefore whosoever heareth these sayings of mine, and doeth them, I will liken him unto a wise man, which built his house upon a rock:

And the rain descended, and the floods came, and the winds blew, and beat upon that house; and it fell not: for it was founded upon a rock.

MATTHEW 7:24–25

If they obey and serve him, they shall spend their days in prosperity, and their years in pleasures.

JOB 36:11

And we know that all things work together for good to them that love God, to them who are the called according to his purpose.

ROMANS 8:28

Parents' Duties

*Bless all parents, God. Give them strength
and love and patience. Use them to
Your glory. Amen.*

For I know him, that he will command his children and his household after him, and they shall keep the way of the LORD, to do justice and judgment; that the LORD may bring upon Abraham that which he hath spoken of him.

GENESIS 18:19

It is in the home that the child learns the basic principle of accountability for actions: first to those around him, and ultimately to God.
—MAXINE HANCOCK

We will not hide them from their children, shewing to the generation to come the praises of the LORD, and his strength, and his wonderful works that he hath done.

For he established a testimony in Jacob, and appointed a law in Israel, which he commanded our fathers, that they should make them known to their children:

That the generation to come might know them, even the children which should be born; who should arise and declare them to their children:

That they might set their hope in God, and not forget the works of God, but keep his commandments.

PSALM 78:4–7

And ye shall teach them your children, speaking of them when thou sittest in thine house, and when thou walkest by the way, when thou liest down, and when thou risest up.

DEUTERONOMY 11:19

And thou shalt shew thy son in that day, saying, This is done because of that which the LORD did unto me when I came forth out of Egypt.

EXODUS 13:8

Only take heed to thyself, and keep thy soul diligently, lest thou forget the things which thine eyes have seen, and lest they depart from thy heart all the days of thy life: but teach them thy sons, and thy sons' sons;

Specially the day that thou stoodest before the LORD thy God in Horeb, when the LORD said unto me, Gather me the people together, and I will make them hear my words, that they may learn to fear me all the days that they shall live upon the earth, and that they may teach their children.

DEUTERONOMY 4:9–10

Train up a child in the way he should go: and when he is old, he will not depart from it.

PROVERBS 22:6

Correct thy son, and he shall give thee rest; yea, he shall give delight unto thy soul.

PROVERBS 29:17

Patience

Lord, being patient isn't easy. I have my agenda for when things should happen—and I'm frustrated and resentful when they don't. Patience will come to me, though, when I'm truly surrendered to You—so here I am, God. Do what You want in my life, in Your time, in Your way. Amen.

Be patient therefore, brethren, unto the coming of the
Lord. Behold, the husbandman waiteth for the precious
fruit of the earth, and hath long patience for it, until he
receive the early and latter rain.

Be ye also patient; stablish your hearts: for the coming of the Lord draweth nigh.

JAMES 5:7–8

For what glory is it, if, when ye be buffeted for your
faults, ye shall take it patiently? but if, when ye do well,
and suffer for it, ye take it patiently, this is acceptable
with God.

1 PETER 2:20

My brethren, count it all joy when ye fall into divers temptations;

Knowing this, that the trying of your faith worketh
patience.

But let patience have her perfect work, that ye may
be perfect and entire, wanting nothing.

JAMES 1:2–4

And let us not be weary in well doing: for in due season
we shall reap, if we faint not.

GALATIANS 6:9

Let us hold fast the profession of our faith without
wavering; (for he is faithful that promised).

HEBREWS 10:23

And not only so, but we glory in tribulations also: knowing that tribulation worketh patience;

And patience, experience; and experience, hope.

ROMANS 5:3–4

But he that shall endure unto the end, the same shall be saved.

MATTHEW 24:13

Be patient with everyone, but above all with thyself. I mean, do not be disheartened by your imperfections, but always rise up with fresh courage.

—FRANCIS DE SALES

That ye be not slothful, but followers of them who through faith and patience inherit the promises.

HEBREWS 6:12

For ye have need of patience, that, after ye have done the will of God, ye might receive the promise.

HEBREWS 10:36

Peace

Thank You, God, for the gift of Your peace.
May it always live in my heart, no matter what
conflict is going on around me. Amen.

And let the peace of God rule in your hearts, to the which also ye are called in one body; and be ye thankful.

COLOSSIANS 3:15

I will hear what God the LORD will speak: for he will speak peace unto his people, and to his saints.

PSALM 85:8

All men desire peace, but few desire the things that make for peace.
—THOMAS Á KEMPIS

And the peace of God, which passeth all understanding, shall keep your hearts and minds through Christ Jesus.

PHILIPPIANS 4:7

Thy faith hath saved thee; go in peace.

LUKE 7:50

Peace I leave with you, my peace I give unto you: not as the world giveth, give I unto you. Let not your heart be troubled, neither let it be afraid.

JOHN 14:27

And the work of righteousness shall be peace; and the

effect of righteousness quietness and assurance for ever.

And my people shall dwell in a peaceable habitation, and in sure dwellings, and in quiet resting places.

ISAIAH 32:17–18

Mark the perfect man, and behold the upright: for the end of that man is peace.

PSALM 37:37

Now the Lord of peace himself give you peace always by all means.

2 THESSALONIANS 3:16

I create the fruit of the lips; Peace, peace to him that is far off, and to him that is near, saith the LORD; and I will heal him.

ISAIAH 57:19

The LORD lift up his countenance upon thee, and give thee peace.

NUMBERS 6:26

Depart from evil, and do good; seek peace, and pursue it.

PSALM 34:14

Moreover I will make a covenant of peace with them; it shall be an everlasting covenant with them: and I will place them, and multiply them, and will set my sanctuary in the midst of them for evermore.

EZEKIEL 37:26

These are the things that ye shall do; Speak ye every man the truth to his neighbour; execute the judgment of truth and peace in your gates.

ZECHARIAH 8:16

To give light to them that sit in darkness and in the shadow of death, to guide our feet into the way of peace.

LUKE 1:79

And I will give peace in the land, and ye shall lie down, and none shall make you afraid: and I will rid evil beasts out of the land, neither shall the sword go through your land.

LEVITICUS 26:6

The LORD will give strength unto his people; the LORD will bless his people with peace.

PSALM 29:11

Prayer

*Dear God, thank You that I can talk with You—
that You are my intimate Friend. I want prayer to
become more and more a part of my life, so that
each and everything I do will be a prayer that
ties me closer to You. Amen.*

Ask, and it shall be given you; seek, and ye shall find; knock, and it shall be opened unto you:

For every one that asketh receiveth; and he that seeketh findeth; and to him that knocketh it shall be opened.

MATTHEW 7:7–8

And all things, whatsoever ye shall ask in prayer, believing, ye shall receive.

MATTHEW 21:22

What is the use of praying if at the very moment of prayer we have so little confidence in God that we are busy planning our own kind of answer to our prayer?
—THOMAS MERTON

He will be very gracious unto thee at the voice of thy cry; when he shall hear it, he will answer thee.

ISAIAH 30:19

Then shall ye call upon me, and ye shall go and pray unto me, and I will hearken unto you.

JEREMIAH 29:12

And this is the confidence that we have in him, that, if we ask anything according to his will, he heareth us:

And if we know that he hear us, whatsoever we ask, we know that we have the petitions that we desired of him.

1 JOHN 5:14–15

And whatsoever ye shall ask in my name, that will I do, that the Father may be glorified in the Son.

If ye shall ask any thing in my name, I will do it.

JOHN 14:13–14

And it shall come to pass, that before they call, I will answer; and while they are yet speaking, I will hear.

ISAIAH 65:24

Whatsoever ye shall ask the Father in my name, he will give it you.

Hitherto have ye asked nothing in my name: ask, and ye shall receive, that your joy may be full.

JOHN 16:23–24

Thou shalt make thy prayer unto him, and he shall hear thee.

JOB 22:27

Confess your faults one to another, and pray one for another, that ye may be healed. The effectual fervent prayer of a righteous man availeth much.

JAMES 5:16

If ye abide in me, and my words abide in you, ye shall ask what ye will, and it shall be done unto you.

JOHN 15:7

But thou, when thou prayest, enter into thy closet, and when thou hast shut thy door, pray to thy Father which is in secret; and thy Father which seeth in secret shall reward thee openly.

MATTHEW 6:6

He shall call upon me, and I will answer him.

PSALM 91:15

The LORD is far from the wicked: but he heareth the prayer of the righteous.

PROVERBS 15:29

O thou that hearest prayer, unto thee shall all flesh come.

PSALM 65:2

Pride

Whatever I have, Lord, You gave to me. I can't take credit for any of it, so how silly I am when I am filled with pride. Amen.

Pride goeth before destruction, and an haughty spirit before a fall.

PROVERBS 16:18

Woe unto them that are wise in their own eyes, and prudent in their own sight!

ISAIAH 5:21

Pride is a kind of pleasure produced by
a man thinking too well of himself.
—BARUCH SPINOZA

Seest thou a man wise in his own conceit? there is more hope of a fool than of him.

PROVERBS 26:12

Look on every one that is proud, and bring him low; and tread down the wicked in their place.

JOB 40:12

The fear of the LORD is to hate evil: pride, and arrogancy, and the evil way, and the froward mouth, do I hate.

PROVERBS 8:13

And he said unto them, Ye are they which justify yourselves before men; but God knoweth your hearts: for that which is highly esteemed among men is abomination in the sight of God.

Luke 16:15

Thou hast rebuked the proud that are cursed, which do err from thy commandments.

Psalm 119:21

But he that glorieth, let him glory in the Lord.

For not he that commendeth himself is approved, but whom the Lord commendeth.

2 Corinthians 10:17–18

Let another man praise thee, and not thine own mouth; a stranger, and not thine own lips.

Proverbs 27:2

An high look, and a proud heart, and the plowing of the wicked, is sin.

Proverbs 21:4

He that is of a proud heart stirreth up strife: but he that putteth his trust in the Lord shall be made fat.

He that trusteth in his own heart is a fool: but whoso walketh wisely, he shall be delivered.

Proverbs 28:25–26

How can ye believe, which receive honour one of another, and seek not the honour that cometh from God only?

John 5:44

And he sat down, and called the twelve, and saith unto

them, If any man desire to be first, the same shall be last of all, and servant of all.

MARK 9:35

A man's pride shall bring him low: but honour shall uphold the humble in spirit.

PROVERBS 29:23

Thy terribleness hath deceived thee, and the pride of thine heart, O thou that dwellest in the clefts of the rock, that holdest the height of the hill: though thou shouldest make thy nest as high as the eagle, I will bring thee down from thence, saith the LORD.

JEREMIAH 49:16

Whoso privily slandereth his neighbour, him will I cut off: him that hath an high look and a proud heart will not I suffer.

PSALM 101:5

The LORD will destroy the house of the proud: but he will establish the border of the widow.

PROVERBS 15:25

Prosperity

Thank You, God, for all that You've given me.
Remind me that the only prosperity that matters
is spiritual prosperity. Amen.

In the day of prosperity be joyful, but in the day of adversity consider: God also hath set the one over against the other, to the end that man should find nothing after him.

ECCLESIASTES 7:14

Let them shout for joy, and be glad, that favour my righteous cause: yea, let them say continually, Let the LORD be magnified, which hath pleasure in the prosperity of his servant.

PSALM 35:27

It is not a sin to have riches, but it is
a sin to fix our hearts upon them.
—JOHN BAPTIST DE LA SALLE

Blessed is the man that walketh not in the counsel of the ungodly, nor standeth in the way of sinners, nor sitteth in the seat of the scornful.

But his delight is in the law of the LORD; and in his law doth he meditate day and night.

And he shall be like a tree planted by the rivers of water, that bringeth forth his fruit in his season; his leaf also shall not wither; and whatsoever he doeth shall prosper.

PSALM 1:1–3

This book of the law shall not depart out of thy mouth; but thou shalt meditate therein day and night, that thou mayest observe to do according to all that is written therein: for then thou shalt make thy way prosperous, and then thou shalt have good success.

JOSHUA 1:8

And the LORD was with him; and he prospered whithersoever he went forth: and he rebelled against the king of Assyria, and served him not.

2 KINGS 18:7

And in every work that he began in the service of the house of God, and in the law, and in the commandments, to seek his God, he did it with all his heart, and prospered.

2 CHRONICLES 31:21

Beloved, I wish above all things that thou mayest prosper and be in health, even as thy soul prospereth.

3 JOHN 1:2

Bring ye all the tithes into the storehouse, that there may be meat in mine house, and prove me now herewith, saith the LORD of hosts, if I will not open you the windows of heaven, and pour you out a blessing, that there shall not be room enough to receive it.

MALACHI 3:10

Protection, God's

Thank You, Lord, for Your protection.
Help me to always rely on You
for my safety. Amen.

The name of the LORD is a strong tower: the righteous runneth into it, and is safe.

PROVERBS 18:10

At destruction and famine thou shalt laugh: neither shalt thou be afraid of the beasts of the earth.

JOB 5:22

And thou shalt be secure, because there is hope; yea, thou shalt dig about thee, and thou shalt take thy rest in safety.

Also thou shalt lie down, and none shall make thee afraid; yea, many shall make suit unto thee.

JOB 11:18–19

The LORD shall preserve thee from all evil: he shall preserve thy soul.

The LORD shall preserve thy going out and thy coming in from this time forth, and even for evermore.

PSALM 121:7–8

And they shall no more be a prey to the heathen, neither shall the beast of the land devour them; but they shall dwell safely, and none shall make them afraid.

EZEKIEL 34:28

When thou liest down, thou shalt not be afraid: yea, thou shalt lie down, and thy sleep shall be sweet.

PROVERBS 3:24

I will both lay me down in peace, and sleep: for thou, LORD, only makest me dwell in safety.

PSALM 4:8

The beloved of the LORD shall dwell in safety by him; and the LORD shall cover him all the day long, and he shall dwell between his shoulders.

DEUTERONOMY 33:12

I am a creature of God, and he has an undoubted right to do with me as seemeth good in his sight.
I rejoice that I am in his hand—that he is everywhere present and can protect me in one place as well as in another.
—ANN HASSELTINE JUDSON

And who is he that will harm you, if ye be followers of that which is good?

1 PETER 3:13

Repentance

*Remind me, Lord, that repentance doesn't
just mean I feel sorry—it means
I change the way I live. Amen.*

The time is fulfilled, and the kingdom of God is at hand: repent ye, and believe the gospel.

MARK 1:15

And they went out, and preached that men should repent.

MARK 6:12

The LORD is nigh unto them that are of a broken heart; and saveth such as be of a contrite spirit.

PSALM 34:18

Repentance was perhaps best defined by a small girl: "It's to be sorry enough to quit."

He healeth the broken in heart, and bindeth up their wounds.

PSALM 147:3

If iniquity be in thine hand, put it far away, and let not wickedness dwell in thy tabernacles.

For then shalt thou lift up thy face without spot; yea, thou shalt be stedfast, and shalt not fear.

JOB 11:14–15

But if the wicked will turn from all his sins that he hath committed, and keep all my statutes, and do that which is lawful and right, he shall surely live, he shall not die.

All his transgressions that he hath committed, they shall not be mentioned unto him: in his righteousness that he hath done he shall live.

EZEKIEL 18:21–22

For I am not come to call the righteous, but sinners to repentance.

MATTHEW 9:13

The Lord is not slack concerning his promise, as some men count slackness; but is longsuffering to us-ward, not willing that any should perish, but that all should come to repentance.

2 PETER 3:9

Repent ye therefore, and be converted, that your sins may be blotted out, when the times of refreshing shall come from the presence of the Lord.

ACTS 3:19

Behold, I stand at the door, and knock: if any man hear my voice, and open the door, I will come in to him, and will sup with him, and he with me.

REVELATION 3:20

Likewise, I say unto you, there is joy in the presence of the angels of God over one sinner that repenteth.

LUKE 15:10

Righteousness

All my righteousness comes from You, God. Thank You for sharing it with me. Remind me never to rely on my own version of righteousness. Amen.

For the LORD God is a sun and shield: the LORD will give grace and glory: no good thing will he withhold from them that walk uprightly.

PSALM 84:11

The young lions do lack, and suffer hunger: but they that seek the LORD shall not want any good thing.

PSALM 34:10

The fear of the wicked, it shall come upon him: but the desire of the righteous shall be granted.

PROVERBS 10:24

Evil pursueth sinners: but to the righteous good shall be repayed.

PROVERBS 13:21

A good man obtaineth favour of the LORD: but a man of wicked devices will he condemn.

PROVERBS 12:2

But seek ye first the kingdom of God, and his righteousness; and all these things shall be added unto you.

MATTHEW 6:33

He that trusteth in his riches shall fall: but the righteous shall flourish as a branch.

PROVERBS 11:28

For thou, LORD, wilt bless the righteous; with favour wilt thou compass him as with a shield.

PSALM 5:12

Salvation belongeth unto the LORD: thy blessing is upon thy people.

PSALM 3:8

He that spared not his own Son, but delivered him up for us all, how shall he not with him also freely give us all things?

ROMANS 8:32

Nothing will do except righteousness;
and no other conception of righteousness
will do, except Christ's conception of it.
—MATTHEW ARNOLD

So that a man shall say, Verily there is a reward for the righteous.

PSALM 58:11

Whether Paul, or Apollos, or Cephas, or the world, or life, or death, or things present, or things to come; all are your's;

And ye are Christ's; and Christ is God's.

1 CORINTHIANS 3:22–23

Say ye to the righteous, that it shall be well with him: for they shall eat the fruit of their doings.

ISAIAH 3:10

Salvation

Because of You, Jesus,
I am eternally safe.
Thank You. Amen.

Therefore if any man be in Christ, he is a new creature: old things are passed away; behold, all things are become new.

2 Corinthians 5:17

But not as the offence, so also is the free gift. For if through the offence of one many be dead, much more the grace of God, and the gift by grace, which is by one man, Jesus Christ, hath abounded unto many.

Romans 5:15

Salvation is not putting a man into Heaven, but putting Heaven into man.
—Maltbie D. Babcock

For he hath made him to be sin for us, who knew no sin; that we might be made the righteousness of God in him.

2 Corinthians 5:21

My little children, these things write I unto you, that ye sin not. And if any man sin, we have an advocate with the Father, Jesus Christ the righteous:

And he is the propitiation for our sins: and not for ours only, but also for the sins of the whole world.

1 John 2:1–2

Jesus answered and said unto him, Verily, verily, I say unto thee, Except a man be born again, he cannot see the kingdom of God.

Nicodemus saith unto him, How can a man be born when he is old? can he enter the second time into his mother's womb, and be born?

Jesus answered, Verily, verily, I say unto thee, Except a man be born of water and of the Spirit, he cannot enter into the kingdom of God.

That which is born of the flesh is flesh; and that which is born of the Spirit is spirit.

Marvel not that I said unto thee, Ye must be born again.

JOHN 3:3–7

For this is good and acceptable in the sight of God our Saviour;

Who will have all men to be saved, and to come unto the knowledge of the truth.

1 TIMOTHY 2:3–4

And you, being dead in your sins and the uncircumcision of your flesh, hath he quickened together with him, having forgiven you all trespasses.

COLOSSIANS 2:13

And you hath he quickened, who were dead in trespasses and sins.

EPHESIANS 2:1

Seeking God

Sometimes, God, You're not very easy to see. Maybe that's because I'm being half-hearted about my seeking. Help me to seek You with my whole heart. Remind me to seek You in everything I do, wherever I am. Amen.

The LORD is with you, while ye be with him; and if ye seek him, he will be found of you; but if ye forsake him, he will forsake you.

2 CHRONICLES 15:2

For thus saith the LORD unto the house of Israel, Seek ye me, and ye shall live.

AMOS 5:4

But if from thence thou shalt seek the LORD thy God, thou shalt find him, if thou seek him with all thy heart and with all thy soul.

DEUTERONOMY 4:29

Sow to yourselves in righteousness, reap in mercy; break up your fallow ground: for it is time to seek the LORD, till he come and rain righteousness upon you.

HOSEA 10:12

But without faith it is impossible to please him: for he that cometh to God must believe that he is, and that he is a rewarder of them that diligently seek him.

HEBREWS 11:6

That they should seek the Lord, if haply they might feel after him, and find him, though he be not far from every one of us.

ACTS 17:27

The hand of our God is upon all them for good that seek him; but his power and his wrath is against all them that forsake him.

EZRA 8:22

The LORD is good unto them that wait for him, to the soul that seeketh him.

LAMENTATIONS 3:25

And thou, Solomon my son, know thou the God of thy father, and serve him with a perfect heart and with a willing mind: for the LORD searcheth all hearts, and understandeth all the imaginations of the thoughts: if thou seek him, he will be found of thee; but if thou forsake him, he will cast thee off for ever.

1 CHRONICLES 28:9

Ever since the days of Adam,
man has been hiding from God and saying,
"God is hard to find."
—FULTON J. SHEEN

If thou wouldest seek unto God betimes, and make thy supplication to the Almighty;

If thou wert pure and upright; surely now he would awake for thee, and make the habitation of thy righteousness prosperous.

JOB 8:5–6

And ye shall seek me, and find me, when ye shall search for me with all your heart.

JEREMIAH 29:13

Self-Righteousness

*Jesus, remove any self-righteousness lurking
in my heart. Remind me that all my righteousness
comes from You. Amen.*

Surely thou hast spoken in mine hearing, and I have heard the voice of thy words, saying,

I am clean without transgression, I am innocent; neither is there iniquity in me.

Thinkest thou this to be right, that thou saidst, My righteousness is more than God's?

JOB 33:8–9, 35:2

*A*s the soul ceases to be "self-regarding" in its activities, it becomes "God-regarding."
—EDWARD LEEN

Woe unto them that are wise in their own eyes, and prudent in their own sight!

ISAIAH 5:21

Surely God will not hear vanity, neither will the Almighty regard it.

JOB 35:13

Seest thou a man wise in his own conceit? there is more hope of a fool than of him.

PROVERBS 26:12

For if a man think himself to be something, when he is nothing, he deceiveth himself.

GALATIANS 6:3

But he that glorieth, let him glory in the Lord.

For not he that commendeth himself is approved, but whom the Lord commendeth.

2 CORINTHIANS 10:17–18

Let another man praise thee, and not thine own mouth; a stranger, and not thine own lips.

PROVERBS 27:2

Jesus said unto them, If ye were blind, ye should have no sin: but now ye say, We see; therefore your sin remaineth.

JOHN 9:41

But we are all as an unclean thing, and all our righteousnesses are as filthy rags; and we all do fade as a leaf; and our iniquities, like the wind, have taken us away.

ISAIAH 64:6

He that is of a proud heart stirreth up strife: but he that putteth his trust in the LORD shall be made fat.

He that trusteth in his own heart is a fool: but whoso walketh wisely, he shall be delivered.

PROVERBS 28:25–26

And he said unto them, Ye are they which justify yourselves before men; but God knoweth your hearts: for that which is highly esteemed among men is abomination in the sight of God.

LUKE 16:15

Sexual Sins

Lord, may I never look at another human being as an object for my gratification. I put my sexuality in Your hands, trusting that You will bring fulfillment to my life, in Your time, in Your way. Amen.

Now the body is not for fornication, but for the Lord; and the Lord for the body.

1 CORINTHIANS 6:13

Flee fornication. Every sin that a man doeth is without the body; but he that committeth fornication sinneth against his own body.

What? know ye not that your body is the temple of the Holy Ghost which is in you, which ye have of God, and ye are not your own?

For ye are bought with a price: therefore glorify God in your body, and in your spirit, which are God's.

1 CORINTHIANS 6:18–20

Now concerning the things whereof ye wrote unto me: It is good for a man not to touch a woman.

1 CORINTHIANS 7:1

I say therefore to the unmarried and widows, It is good for them if they abide even as I.

But if they cannot contain, let them marry: for it is better to marry than to burn.

1 CORINTHIANS 7:8–9

Nevertheless he that standeth stedfast in his heart, having no necessity, but hath power over his own will, and hath so decreed in his heart that he will keep his virgin, doeth well.

1 CORINTHIANS 7:37

Marriage is honourable in all, and the bed undefiled: but whoremongers and adulterers God will judge.

HEBREWS 13:4

For this is the will of God, even your sanctification, that ye should abstain from fornication.

1 Thessalonians 4:3

Where there is an ongoing relationship of caring. Where there is a sense of humor. Where there is a sense of mutual mercy. Where there is a sense that God has given sex to you. . .there is nothing livelier. But when it is merchandised as a commodity for instant gratification, there is nothing deadlier than sex.
—William Swing

The Lord knoweth how to deliver the godly out of temptations, and to reserve the unjust unto the day of judgment to be punished.

2 Peter 2:9

Shame

*Thank You, Jesus, for washing all
my shame away. Amen.*

For the scripture saith, Whosoever believeth on him shall not be ashamed.

ROMANS 10:11

Then shall I not be ashamed, when I have respect unto all thy commandments.

PSALM 119:6

Experiences of shame appear to embody
the root meaning of the word—to uncover, to
expose, to wound. They are experiences
of exposure. . . .
The exposure may be to others, but whether
others are or are not involved, it is always. . .
exposure to one's own eyes.
—HELEN MERREL LYND

And hope maketh not ashamed; because the love of God is shed abroad in our hearts by the Holy Ghost which is given unto us.

ROMANS 5:5

Study to shew thyself approved unto God, a workman that needeth not to be ashamed, rightly dividing the word of truth.

2 TIMOTHY 2:15

For the which cause I also suffer these things: nevertheless I am not ashamed: for I know whom I have believed, and am persuaded that he is able to keep that which I have committed unto him against that day.

2 TIMOTHY 1:12

As it is written, Behold, I lay in Sion a stumblingstone and rock of offence: and whosoever believeth on him shall not be ashamed.

ROMANS 9:33

Let my heart be sound in thy statutes; that I be not ashamed.

PSALM 119:80

Yet if any man suffer as a Christian, let him not be ashamed; but let him glorify God on this behalf.

1 PETER 4:16

Fear not; for thou shalt not be ashamed: neither be thou confounded; for thou shalt not be put to shame: for thou shalt forget the shame of thy youth, and shalt not remember the reproach of thy widowhood any more.

ISAIAH 54:4

And now, little children, abide in him; that, when he shall appear, we may have confidence, and not be ashamed before him at his coming.

1 JOHN 2:28

Sin, Freedom from

*Thank You, Jesus, for making
me whole. Amen.*

Then will I sprinkle clean water upon you, and ye shall be clean: from all your filthiness, and from all your idols, will I cleanse you.

A new heart also will I give you, and a new spirit will I put within you: and I will take away the stony heart out of your flesh, and I will give you an heart of flesh.

EZEKIEL 36:25–26

To him give all the prophets witness, that through his name whosoever believeth in him shall receive remission of sins.

ACTS 10:43

Knowing this, that our old man is crucified with him, that the body of sin might be destroyed, that henceforth we should not serve sin.

For he that is dead is freed from sin.

ROMANS 6:6–7

Therefore if any man be in Christ, he is a new creature: old things are passed away; behold, all things are become new.

2 CORINTHIANS 5:17

What shall we say then? Shall we continue in sin, that grace may abound?

God forbid. How shall we, that are dead to sin, live any longer therein?

ROMANS 6:1–2

Likewise reckon ye also yourselves to be dead indeed unto sin, but alive unto God through Jesus Christ our Lord.

ROMANS 6:11

And she shall bring forth a son, and thou shalt call his name JESUS: for he shall save his people from their sins.

MATTHEW 1:21

Be it known unto you therefore, men and brethren, that through this man is preached unto you the forgiveness of sins.

ACTS 13:38

Salvation consists in passing from this dark, restless and tormented Existence in which the worldly man lives, to live in truth, to that in which it is really worth living.
—CATHERINE OF SIENA

Who gave himself for our sins, that he might deliver us from this present evil world, according to the will of God and our Father.

GALATIANS 1:4

And if any man sin, we have an advocate with the Father, Jesus Christ the righteous:

And he is the propitiation for our sins: and not for ours only, but also for the sins of the whole world.

1 JOHN 2:1–2

Who his own self bare our sins in his own body on the tree, that we, being dead to sins, should live unto righteousness: by whose stripes ye were healed.

1 Peter 2:24

This is a faithful saying, and worthy of all acceptation, that Christ Jesus came into the world to save sinners; of whom I am chief.

1 Timothy 1:15

And ye know that he was manifested to take away our sins; and in him is no sin.

1 John 3:5

For by one offering he hath perfected for ever them that are sanctified.

Hebrews 10:14

The next day John seeth Jesus coming unto him, and saith, Behold the Lamb of God, which taketh away the sin of the world.

John 1:29

In whom we have redemption through his blood, the forgiveness of sins, according to the riches of his grace.

Ephesians 1:7

But he was wounded for our transgressions, he was bruised for our iniquities: the chastisement of our peace was upon him; and with his stripes we are healed.

Isaiah 53:5

Spiritual Growth

*God, may I keep growing closer and closer to You,
more and more like Your Son. Amen.*

Herein is my Father glorified, that ye bear much fruit; so shall ye be my disciples.

JOHN 15:8

And beside this, giving all diligence, add to your faith virtue; and to virtue knowledge.

2 PETER 1:5

And this I pray, that your love may abound yet more and more in knowledge and in all judgment.

PHILIPPIANS 1:9

Being filled with the fruits of righteousness, which are by Jesus Christ, unto the glory and praise of God.

PHILIPPIANS 1:11

The righteous also shall hold on his way, and he that hath clean hands shall be stronger and stronger.

JOB 17:9

Furthermore then we beseech you, brethren, and exhort you by the Lord Jesus, that as ye have received of us how ye ought to walk and to please God, so ye would abound more and more.

1 THESSALONIANS 4:1

But we all, with open face beholding as in a glass the glory of the Lord, are changed into the same image from glory to glory, even as by the Spirit of the Lord.

2 CORINTHIANS 3:18

The LORD will perfect that which concerneth me: thy

mercy, O Lord, endureth for ever: forsake not the works of thine own hands.

PSALM 138:8

Which is come unto you, as it is in all the world; and bringeth forth fruit, as it doth also in you, since the day ye heard of it, and knew the grace of God in truth.

COLOSSIANS 1:6

I have come upon the happy discovery that this life hid with Christ in God is a continuous unfolding.
—EUGENIA PRICE

We are bound to thank God always for you, brethren, as it is meet, because that your faith groweth exceedingly, and the charity of every one of you all toward each other aboundeth.

2 THESSALONIANS 1:3

But the path of the just is as the shining light, that shineth more and more unto the perfect day.

PROVERBS 4:18

Success

*Thank You for blessing me in so many ways, Father.
I know that only with You will I find true
success in my life. Amen.*

In the house of the righteous is much treasure: but in the revenues of the wicked is trouble.

PROVERBS 15:6

By humility and the fear of the LORD are riches, and honour, and life.

PROVERBS 22:4

What definition did Jesus give of "success"? He said that true success is. . .to attain to eternal life; all else is failure.
—TOYOHIKO KAGAWA

And the LORD thy God will make thee plenteous in every work of thine hand, in the fruit of thy body, and in the fruit of thy cattle, and in the fruit of thy land, for good: for the LORD will again rejoice over thee for good, as he rejoiced over thy fathers.

DEUTERONOMY 30:9

Then shall he give the rain of thy seed, that thou shalt sow the ground withal; and bread of the increase of the earth, and it shall be fat and plenteous: in that day shall thy cattle feed in large pastures.

ISAIAH 30:23

And the LORD shall make thee plenteous in goods, in the fruit of thy body, and in the fruit of thy cattle, and in the fruit of thy ground, in the land which the LORD sware unto thy fathers to give thee.

The LORD shall open unto thee his good treasure, the heaven to give the rain unto thy land in his season, and to bless all the work of thine hand: and thou shalt lend unto many nations, and thou shalt not borrow.

And the LORD shall make thee the head, and not the tail; and thou shalt be above only, and thou shalt not be beneath; if that thou hearken unto the commandments of the LORD thy God, which I command thee this day, to observe and to do them.

DEUTERONOMY 28:11–13

Every man also to whom God hath given riches and wealth, and hath given him power to eat thereof, and to take his portion, and to rejoice in his labour; this is the gift of God.

ECCLESIASTES 5:19

And also that every man should eat and drink, and enjoy the good of all his labour, it is the gift of God.

ECCLESIASTES 3:13

Thou shalt also decree a thing, and it shall be established unto thee: and the light shall shine upon thy ways.

JOB 22:28

Riches and honour are with me; yea, durable riches and righteousness.

My fruit is better than gold, yea, than fine gold; and my revenue than choice silver.

PROVERBS 8:18–19

Temptation

*Teach me, God, when I feel tempted to run immediately
to You, so that each temptation becomes the point
where I immediately draw near to You, a knot that
ties me even closer to Your presence. Amen.*

For we have not an high priest which cannot be touched with the feeling of our infirmities; but was in all points tempted like as we are, yet without sin.

Let us therefore come boldly unto the throne of grace, that we may obtain mercy, and find grace to help in time of need.

HEBREWS 4:15–16

Dearly beloved, I beseech you as strangers and pilgrims, abstain from fleshly lusts, which war against the soul.

1 PETER 2:11

This I say then, Walk in the Spirit, and ye shall not fulfil the lust of the flesh.

For the flesh lusteth against the Spirit, and the Spirit against the flesh: and these are contrary the one to the other: so that ye cannot do the things that ye would.

GALATIANS 5:16–17

Blessed is the man that endureth temptation: for when he is tried, he shall receive the crown of life, which the Lord hath promised to them that love him.

Let no man say when he is tempted, I am tempted of God: for God cannot be tempted with evil, neither tempteth he any man.

JAMES 1:12–13

For the grace of God has been revealed, bringing salvation to all people. And we are instructed to turn from godless living and sinful pleasures. We should live in this evil world with self-control, right conduct, and devotion to God, while we look forward to that wonderful event when the glory of our great God and Savior, Jesus Christ, will be revealed. He gave his life to free us from every kind of sin, to cleanse us, and to make us his very own people, totally committed to doing what is right.

Titus 2:11–14 NLT

One great mistake we make about temptation is to feel as if the time spent in enduring them was all lost time. Days pass, perhaps, and we have been so beset with temptations as to feel we have made no progress. But it often happens that we have been serving the Lord far more truly while thus "continuing with him" in temptation, than we could have in our times of comparative freedom from it.

—Hannah Whitall Smith

Thankfulness

*Thank You, God, for all the ways You bless me
every day. May I always have
a thankful heart. Amen.*

Offer unto God thanksgiving; and pay thy vows unto the most High.

PSALM 50:14

Let us come before his presence with thanksgiving, and make a joyful noise unto him with psalms.

PSALM 95:2

Now thank we all our God,
With heart and hands and voices.
Who wondrous things hath done
in whom his world rejoices.
—CATHERINE WINKWORTH

Enter into his gates with thanksgiving, and into his courts with praise: be thankful unto him, and bless his name.

PSALM 100:4

Being enriched in every thing to all bountifulness, which causeth through us thanksgiving to God.

2 CORINTHIANS 9:11

Be careful for nothing; but in every thing by prayer and supplication with thanksgiving let your requests be made known unto God.

PHILIPPIANS 4:6

Continue in prayer, and watch in the same with thanksgiving.

COLOSSIANS 4:2

Saying, Amen: Blessing, and glory, and wisdom, and thanksgiving, and honour, and power, and might, be unto our God for ever and ever. Amen.

REVELATION 7:12

By him therefore let us offer the sacrifice of praise to God continually, that is, the fruit of our lips giving thanks to his name.

HEBREWS 13:15

Thanks be unto God for his unspeakable gift.

2 CORINTHIANS 9:15

Now thanks be unto God, which always causeth us to triumph in Christ, and maketh manifest the savour of his knowledge by us in every place.

2 CORINTHIANS 2:14

I thank thee, and praise thee, O thou God of my fathers, who hast given me wisdom and might, and hast made known unto me now what we desired of thee: for thou hast now made known unto us the king's matter.

DANIEL 2:23

Trials

*May I see Your light, Lord, even in life's
broken pieces. I trust You. Amen.*

That the trial of your faith, being much more precious than of gold that perisheth, though it be tried with fire, might be found unto praise and honour and glory at the appearing of Jesus Christ.

1 PETER 1:7

Hear me, O LORD; for thy lovingkindness is good: turn unto me according to the multitude of thy tender mercies.

And hide not thy face from thy servant; for I am in trouble: hear me speedily.

PSALM 69:16–17

My flesh and my heart faileth: but God is the strength of my heart, and my portion for ever.

PSALM 73:26

Blessed be God, even the Father of our Lord Jesus Christ, the Father of mercies, and the God of all comfort;

Who comforteth us in all our tribulation, that we may be able to comfort them which are in any trouble, by the comfort wherewith we ourselves are comforted of God.

2 CORINTHIANS 1:3–4

Who shall separate us from the love of Christ? shall tribulation, or distress, or persecution, or famine, or nakedness, or peril, or sword?

Nay, in all these things we are more than conquerors through him that loved us.

ROMANS 8:35, 37

These things I have spoken unto you, that in me ye might have peace. In the world ye shall have tribulation: but be of good cheer; I have overcome the world.

JOHN 16:33

In the day of prosperity be joyful, but in the day of adversity consider: God also hath set the one over against the other, to the end that man should find nothing after him.

ECCLESIASTES 7:14

Gideon's lamps were revealed when his soldiers' pitchers were broken. If our pitchers are broken for the Lord and His gospel's sake, lamps will be revealed that otherwise would have stayed hidden and unseen. . . .Out of affliction's dark comes spiritual light.
—JOHN BUNYAN

If thou faint in the day of adversity, thy strength is small.

PROVERBS 24:10

Be not far from me; for trouble is near; for there is none to help.

PSALM 22:11

God is our refuge and strength, a very present help in trouble.

PSALM 46:1

From the end of the earth will I cry unto thee, when my heart is overwhelmed: lead me to the rock that is higher than I.

PSALM 61:2

And we know that all things work together for good to them that love God, to them who are the called according to his purpose.

ROMANS 8:28

He shall not be afraid of evil tidings: his heart is fixed, trusting in the LORD.

PSALM 112:7

Although the fig tree shall not blossom, neither shall fruit be in the vines; the labour of the olive shall fail, and the fields shall yield no meat; the flock shall be cut off from the fold, and there shall be no herd in the stalls:

Yet I will rejoice in the LORD, I will joy in the God of my salvation.

HABAKKUK 3:17–18

Trust

*Lord, You know that sometimes I'm filled with doubts.
But even then, I commit myself to You. I'm trusting You
to handle everything that happens to me. Amen.*

God is our refuge and strength, a very present help in trouble.

Therefore will not we fear, though the earth be removed, and though the mountains be carried into the midst of the sea.

PSALM 46:1–2

Fear not, little flock; for it is your Father's good pleasure to give you the kingdom.

LUKE 12:32

For the LORD God is a sun and shield: the LORD will give grace and glory: no good thing will he withhold from them that walk uprightly.

O LORD of hosts, blessed is the man that trusteth in thee.

PSALM 84:11–12

Trust in the LORD, and do good; so shalt thou dwell in the land, and verily thou shalt be fed.

Delight thyself also in the LORD; and he shall give thee the desires of thine heart.

Commit thy way unto the LORD; trust also in him; and he shall bring it to pass.

PSALM 37:3–5

Trust in the LORD with all thine heart; and lean not unto thine own understanding.

In all thy ways acknowledge him, and he shall direct thy paths.

PROVERBS 3:5–6

They that trust in the LORD shall be as mount Zion, which cannot be removed, but abideth for ever.

PSALM 125:1

Therefore take no thought, saying, What shall we eat? or, What shall we drink? or, Wherewithal shall we be clothed?

(For after all these things do the Gentiles seek:) for your heavenly Father knoweth that ye have need of all these things.

MATTHEW 6:31–32

Can anyone think of believing in God without trusting Him? Is it possible to trust in God for the big things like forgiveness and eternal life, and then refuse to trust Him for the little things like clothing and food?
—OSWALD C. J. HOFFMAN

Casting all your care upon him; for he careth for you.

1 PETER 5:7

Blessed is that man that maketh the LORD his trust.

PSALM 40:4

The LORD recompense thy work, and a full reward be given thee of the LORD God of Israel, under whose wings thou art come to trust.

RUTH 2:12

The God of my rock; in him will I trust: he is my shield, and the horn of my salvation, my high tower, and my refuge, my saviour; thou savest me from violence.

2 SAMUEL 22:3

Though he slay me, yet will I trust in him: but I will maintain mine own ways before him.

JOB 13:15

Thou wilt keep him in perfect peace, whose mind is stayed on thee: because he trusteth in thee.

Trust ye in the LORD for ever: for in the LORD JEHOVAH is everlasting strength.

ISAIAH 26:3–4

Behold, God is my salvation; I will trust, and not be afraid: for the LORD JEHOVAH is my strength and my song; he also is become my salvation.

ISAIAH 12:2

The LORD is good, a strong hold in the day of trouble; and he knoweth them that trust in him.

NAHUM 1:7

Wisdom

Lord, give me Your wisdom. Help me to know the difference between the world's sort of wisdom and the wisdom that comes from Your Spirit. Amen.

If any of you lack wisdom, let him ask of God, that giveth to all men liberally, and upbraideth not; and it shall be given him.

JAMES 1:5

And he will teach us of his ways, and we will walk in his paths.

ISAIAH 2:3

I will instruct thee and teach thee in the way which thou shalt go: I will guide thee with mine eye.

PSALM 32:8

For God giveth to a man that is good in his sight wisdom, and knowledge, and joy.

ECCLESIASTES 2:26

I will bless the LORD who guides me; even at night my heart instructs me.

PSALM 16:7 NLT

And we know that the Son of God is come, and hath given us an understanding, that we may know him that is true, and we are in him that is true, even in his Son Jesus Christ. This is the true God, and eternal life.

1 JOHN 5:20

Evil men understand not judgment: but they that seek the LORD understand all things.

PROVERBS 28:5

Then shalt thou understand the fear of the LORD, and

find the knowledge of God.

For the LORD giveth wisdom: out of his mouth cometh knowledge and understanding.

He layeth up sound wisdom for the righteous: he is a buckler to them that walk uprightly.

PROVERBS 2:5–7

All the wisdom in the world and all human cleverness compared with the infinite wisdom of God is sheer and extreme ignorance.
—JOHN OF THE CROSS

For God, who commanded the light to shine out of darkness, hath shined in our hearts, to give the light of the knowledge of the glory of God in the face of Jesus Christ.

2 CORINTHIANS 4:6

Behold, thou desirest truth in the inward parts: and in the hidden part thou shalt make me to know wisdom.

PSALM 51:6

The law of the LORD is perfect, converting the soul: the testimony of the LORD is sure, making wise the simple.

PSALM 19:7

Wisdom and knowledge is granted unto thee; and I will

give thee riches, and wealth, and honour, such as none of the kings have had that have been before thee, neither shall there any after thee have the like.

2 CHRONICLES 1:12

A wise man will hear, and will increase learning; and a man of understanding shall attain unto wise counsels.

PROVERBS 1:5

I thank thee, and praise thee, O thou God of my fathers, who hast given me wisdom and might, and hast made known unto me now what we desired of thee: for thou hast now made known unto us the king's matter.

DANIEL 2:23

For this cause we also, since the day we heard it, do not cease to pray for you, and to desire that ye might be filled with the knowledge of his will in all wisdom and spiritual understanding.

COLOSSIANS 1:9

If any of you lack wisdom, let him ask of God, that giveth to all men liberally, and upbraideth not; and it shall be given him.

JAMES 1:5

And that from a child thou hast known the holy scriptures, which are able to make thee wise unto salvation through faith which is in Christ Jesus.

2 TIMOTHY 3:15

And I have filled him with the spirit of God, in wisdom,

and in understanding, and in knowledge, and in all manner of workmanship.

Exodus 31:3

With him is wisdom and strength, he hath counsel and understanding.

Job 12:13

And unto man he said, Behold, the fear of the Lord, that is wisdom; and to depart from evil is understanding.

Job 28:28

How much better is it to get wisdom than gold! and to get understanding rather to be chosen than silver!

Proverbs 16:16

And the spirit of the Lord shall rest upon him, the spirit of wisdom and understanding, the spirit of counsel and might, the spirit of knowledge and of the fear of the Lord.

Isaiah 11:2

Trust in the Lord with all thine heart; and lean not unto thine own understanding.

Proverbs 3:5

But the wisdom that is from above is first pure, then peaceable, gentle, and easy to be entreated, full of mercy and good fruits, without partiality, and without hypocrisy.

James 3:17

For wisdom is a defence, and money is a defence: but

the excellency of knowledge is, that wisdom giveth life
to them that have it.

ECCLESIASTES 7:12

All the wisdom of the world is childish
foolishness in comparison with the
acknowledgment of Jesus Christ.
—MARTIN LUTHER

Then said I, Wisdom is better than strength: nevertheless the poor man's wisdom is despised, and his words
are not heard.

The words of wise men are heard in quiet more than
the cry of him that ruleth among fools.

Wisdom is better than weapons of war: but one sinner destroyeth much good.

ECCLESIASTES 9:16–18

Word of God

Thank You, Christ, for showing us Yourself
in Your Word. Remind me to daily take advantage
of this revelation. Amen.

For I am not ashamed of the gospel of Christ: for it is the power of God unto salvation to every one that believeth; to the Jew first, and also to the Greek.

ROMANS 1:16

Blessed is he that readeth, and they that hear the words of this prophecy, and keep those things which are written therein: for the time is at hand.

REVELATION 1:3

We have also a more sure word of prophecy; whereunto ye do well that ye take heed, as unto a light that shineth in a dark place, until the day dawn, and the day star arise in your hearts.

2 PETER 1:19

For the word of God is quick, and powerful, and sharper than any twoedged sword, piercing even to the dividing asunder of soul and spirit, and of the joints and marrow, and is a discerner of the thoughts and intents of the heart.

HEBREWS 4:12

The entrance of thy words giveth light; it giveth understanding unto the simple.

PSALM 119:130

For the commandment is a lamp; and the law is light; and reproofs of instruction are the way of life.

PROVERBS 6:23

Thy word is a lamp unto my feet, and a light unto my path.

PSALM 119:105

Search the scriptures; for in them ye think ye have eternal life: and they are they which testify of me.

JOHN 5:39

And that from a child thou hast known the holy scriptures, which are able to make thee wise unto salvation through faith which is in Christ Jesus.

All scripture is given by inspiration of God, and is profitable for doctrine, for reproof, for correction, for instruction in righteousness.

2 TIMOTHY 3:15–16

Other books were given for our information, the Bible was given for our transformation.

—ANONYMOUS

So then faith cometh by hearing, and hearing by the word of God.

ROMANS 10:17

As newborn babes, desire the sincere milk of the word, that ye may grow thereby.

1 PETER 2:2

Wherefore lay apart all filthiness and superfluity of naughtiness, and receive with meekness the engrafted word, which is able to save your souls.

But be ye doers of the word, and not hearers only, deceiving your own selves.

For if any be a hearer of the word, and not a doer, he is like unto a man beholding his natural face in a glass:

For he beholdeth himself, and goeth his way, and straightway forgetteth what manner of man he was.

But whoso looketh into the perfect law of liberty, and continueth therein, he being not a forgetful hearer, but a doer of the work, this man shall be blessed in his deed.

JAMES 1:21–25

Therefore shall ye lay up these my words in your heart and in your soul, and bind them for a sign upon your hand, that they may be as frontlets between your eyes.

DEUTERONOMY 11:18

Work

*Father, be glorified in my work. Thank You for it,
the parts I like, the parts that bore me, the parts
I hate. Use all of it, even the trivial parts,
to reveal Yourself in my world. Amen.*

And God blessed the seventh day, and sanctified it: because that in it he had rested from all his work which God created and made.

GENESIS 2:3

The LORD shall open unto thee his good treasure, the heaven to give the rain unto thy land in his season, and to bless all the work of thine hand: and thou shalt lend unto many nations, and thou shalt not borrow.

DEUTERONOMY 28:12

Be ye strong therefore, and let not your hands be weak: for your work shall be rewarded.

2 CHRONICLES 15:7

And in every work that he began in the service of the house of God, and in the law, and in the commandments, to seek his God, he did it with all his heart, and prospered.

2 CHRONICLES 31:21

Even a child is known by his doings, whether his work be pure, and whether it be right.

PROVERBS 20:11

Jesus saith unto them, My meat is to do the will of him that sent me, and to finish his work.

JOHN 4:34

In all labour there is profit: but the talk of the lips tendeth only to penury.

PROVERBS 14:23

Then said they unto him, What shall we do, that we might work the works of God?

Jesus answered and said unto them, This is the work of God, that ye believe on him whom he hath sent.

JOHN 6:28–29

I have glorified thee on the earth: I have finished the work which thou gavest me to do.

And now, O Father, glorify thou me with thine own self with the glory which I had with thee before the world was.

JOHN 17:4–5

He who labors as he prays
lifts his heart to God with his hands.
—BERNARD OF CLAIRVAUX

Therefore, my beloved brethren, be ye stedfast, unmoveable, always abounding in the work of the Lord, forasmuch as ye know that your labour is not in vain in the Lord.

1 CORINTHIANS 15:58

That ye might walk worthy of the Lord unto all pleasing, being fruitful in every good work, and increasing in the knowledge of God.

COLOSSIANS 1:10

For we hear that there are some which walk among you disorderly, working not at all, but are busybodies.

Now them that are such we command and exhort by our Lord Jesus Christ, that with quietness they work, and eat their own bread.

2 Thessalonians 3:11–12

For God is not unrighteous to forget your work and labour of love, which ye have shewed toward his name, in that ye have ministered to the saints, and do minister.

And we desire that every one of you do shew the same diligence to the full assurance of hope unto the end.

Hebrews 6:10–11

Except the Lord build the house, they labour in vain that build it: except the Lord keep the city, the watchman waketh but in vain.

Psalm 127:1

Let him that stole steal no more: but rather let him labour, working with his hands the thing which is good, that he may have to give to him that needeth.

Ephesians 4:28

Worry

Dear God, You know how easily I fall into worrying.
Teach me to catch my worries before they run away
with me—and then give them to You. If my life is in
Your hands, then I have nothing to fear. Amen.

Be careful for nothing; but in every thing by prayer and supplication with thanksgiving let your requests be made known unto God.

And the peace of God, which passeth all understanding, shall keep your hearts and minds through Christ Jesus.

PHILIPPIANS 4:6–7

God is our refuge and strength, a very present help in trouble.

Therefore will not we fear, though the earth be removed, and though the mountains be carried into the midst of the sea;

Though the waters thereof roar and be troubled, though the mountains shake with the swelling thereof. Selah.

PSALM 46:1–3

But my God shall supply all your need according to his riches in glory by Christ Jesus.

PHILIPPIANS 4:19

For he shall be as a tree planted by the waters, and that spreadeth out her roots by the river, and shall not see when heat cometh, but her leaf shall be green; and shall not be careful in the year of drought, neither shall cease from yielding fruit.

JEREMIAH 17:8

And Jesus answered and said unto her, Martha, Martha, thou art careful and troubled about many things:

But one thing is needful: and Mary hath chosen that

good part, which shall not be taken away from her.

LUKE 10:41–42

The LORD also will be a refuge for the oppressed, a refuge in times of trouble.

And they that know thy name will put their trust in thee: for thou, LORD, hast not forsaken them that seek thee.

PSALM 9:9–10

Thou art my hiding place; thou shalt preserve me from trouble; thou shalt compass me about with songs of deliverance. Selah.

PSALM 32:7

Fretting springs from a determination
to get our own way.
—OSWALD CHAMBERS

He shall call upon me, and I will answer him: I will be with him in trouble; I will deliver him, and honour him.

PSALM 91:15

Worship

I don't have enough words to praise You, Lord.
You are beyond my ability to understand or express.
I can only worship You in my heart, lifting
my life up to You. Amen.

All the earth shall worship thee, and shall sing unto thee; they shall sing to thy name. Selah.

PSALM 66:4

O come, let us worship and bow down: let us kneel before the LORD our maker.

For he is our God; and we are the people of his pasture, and the sheep of his hand. To day if ye will hear his voice.

PSALM 95:6–7

All true and acceptable worship to God is offered in the inward and immediate moving and drawing of His own Spirit, which is neither limited to places, times, or persons.
—ROBERT BARCLAY

Exalt the LORD our God, and worship at his holy hill; for the LORD our God is holy.

PSALM 99:9

Now when Jesus was born in Bethlehem of Judaea in the days of Herod the king, behold, there came wise men from the east to Jerusalem,

Saying, Where is he that is born King of the Jews?

for we have seen his star in the east, and are come to worship him.

MATTHEW 2:1–2

God is a Spirit: and they that worship him must worship him in spirit and in truth.

JOHN 4:24

The four and twenty elders fall down before him that sat on the throne, and worship him that liveth for ever and ever, and cast their crowns before the throne, saying,

Thou art worthy, O Lord, to receive glory and honour and power: for thou hast created all things, and for thy pleasure they are and were created.

REVELATION 4:10–11

All nations whom thou hast made shall come and worship before thee, O Lord; and shall glorify thy name.

PSALM 86:9

Who shall not fear thee, O Lord, and glorify thy name? for thou only art holy: for all nations shall come and worship before thee; for thy judgments are made manifest.

REVELATION 15:4

And I fell at his feet to worship him. And he said unto me, See thou do it not: I am thy fellowservant, and of thy brethren that have the testimony of Jesus: worship God: for the testimony of Jesus is the spirit of prophecy.

REVELATION 19:10

And the devil said unto him, All this power will I give thee, and the glory of them: for that is delivered unto me; and to whomsoever I will I give it.

If thou therefore wilt worship me, all shall be thine.

And Jesus answered and said unto him, Get thee behind me, Satan: for it is written, Thou shalt worship the Lord thy God, and him only shalt thou serve.

LUKE 4:6–8

And, behold, there came a leper and worshipped him, saying, Lord, if thou wilt, thou canst make me clean.

And Jesus put forth his hand, and touched him, saying, I will; be thou clean. And immediately his leprosy was cleansed.

MATTHEW 8:2–3

And the four and twenty elders, which sat before God on their seats, fell upon their faces, and worshipped God,

Saying, We give thee thanks, O Lord God Almighty, which art, and wast, and art to come; because thou hast taken to thee thy great power, and hast reigned.

REVELATION 11:16–17

Schedule for Reading Through the Bible in a Year

Bible Readings for January

January 1 - Luke 5:27–39, Genesis 1–2, Psalm 1
January 2 - Luke 6:1–26, Genesis 3–5, Psalm 2
January 3 - Luke 6:27–49, Genesis 6–7, Psalm 3
January 4 - Luke 7:1–17, Genesis 8–10, Psalm 4
January 5 - Luke 7:18–50, Genesis 11, Psalm 5
January 6 - Luke 8:1–25, Genesis 12, Psalm 6
January 7 - Luke 8:26–56, Genesis 13–14, Psalm 7
January 8 - Luke 9:1–27, Genesis 15, Psalm 8
January 9 - Luke 9:28–62, Genesis 16, Psalm 9
January 10 - Luke 10:1–20, Genesis 17, Psalm 10
January 11 - Luke 10:21–42, Genesis 18, Psalm 11
January 12 - Luke 11:1–28, Genesis 19, Psalm 12
January 13 - Luke 11:29–54, Genesis 20, Psalm 13
January 14 - Luke 12:1–31, Genesis 21, Psalm 14
January 15 - Luke 12:32–59, Genesis 22, Psalm 15
January 16 - Luke 13:1–17, Genesis 23, Psalm 16
January 17 - Luke 13:18–35, Genesis 24, Psalm 17
January 18 - Luke 14:1–24, Genesis 25, Psalm 18
January 19 - Luke 14:25–35, Genesis 26, Psalm 19
January 20 - Luke 15, Genesis 27:1–45, Psalm 20
January 21 - Luke 16, Genesis 27:46–28:22, Psalm 21
January 22 - Luke 17, Genesis 29:1–30, Psalm 22
January 23 - Luke 18:1–17, Genesis 29:31–30:43, Psalm 23
January 24 - Luke 18:18–43, Genesis 31, Psalm 24
January 25 - Luke 19:1–27, Genesis 32–33, Psalm 25
January 26 - Luke 19:28–48, Genesis 34, Psalm 26
January 27 - Luke 20:1–26, Genesis 35–36, Psalm 27
January 28 - Luke 20:27–47, Genesis 37, Psalm 28
January 29 - Luke 21, Genesis 38, Psalm 29
January 30 - Luke 22:1–38, Genesis 39, Psalm 30
January 31 - Luke 22:39–71, Genesis 40, Psalm 31

Bible Readings for February

February 1 - Luke 23:1–25, Genesis 41, Psalm 32
February 2 - Luke 23:26–56, Genesis 42, Psalm 33
February 3 - Luke 24:1–12, Genesis 43, Psalm 34
February 4 - Luke 24:13–53, Genesis 44, Psalm 35
February 5 - Hebrews 1, Genesis 45:1–46:27, Psalm 36
February 6 - Hebrews 2, Genesis 46:28–47:31, Psalm 37
February 7 - Hebrews 3:1–4:13, Genesis 48, Psalm 38
February 8 - Hebrews 4:14–6:12, Genesis 49–50, Psalm 39
February 9 - Hebrews 6:13–20, Exodus 1–2, Psalm 40
February 10 - Hebrews 7, Exodus 3–4, Psalm 41
February 11 - Hebrews 8, Exodus 5:1–6:27, Proverbs 1
February 12 - Hebrews 9:1–22, Exodus 6:28–8:32, Proverbs 2
February 13 - Hebrews 9:23–10:18, Exodus 9–10, Proverbs 3
February 14 - Hebrews 10:19–39, Exodus 11–12, Proverbs 4
February 15 - Hebrews 11:1–22, Exodus 13–14, Proverbs 5
February 16 - Hebrews 11:23–40, Exodus 15, Proverbs 6:1–7:5
February 17 - Hebrews 12, Exodus 16–17, Proverbs 7:6–27
February 18 - Hebrews 13, Exodus 18–19, Proverbs 8
February 19 - Matthew 1, Exodus 20–21, Proverbs 9
February 20 - Matthew 2, Exodus 22–23, Proverbs 10
February 21 - Matthew 3, Exodus 24, Proverbs 11
February 22 - Matthew 4, Exodus 25–27, Proverbs 12
February 23 - Matthew 5:1–20, Exodus 28–29, Proverbs 13
February 24 - Matthew 5:21–48, Exodus 30–32, Proverbs 14
February 25 - Matthew 6:1–18, Exodus 33–34, Proverbs 15
February 26 - Matthew 6:19–34, Exodus 35–36, Proverbs 16
February 27 - Matthew 7, Exodus 37–38, Proverbs 17
February 28 - Matthew 8:1–13, Exodus 39–40, Proverbs 18

Bible Readings for March

March 1 - Matthew 8:14–34, Leviticus 1–2, Proverbs 19
March 2 - Matthew 9:1–17, Leviticus 3–4, Proverbs 20
March 3 - Matthew 9:18–38, Leviticus 5–6, Proverbs 21
March 4 - Matthew 10:1–25, Leviticus 7–8, Proverbs 22
March 5 - Matthew 10:26–42, Leviticus 9–10, Proverbs 23
March 6 - Matthew 11:1–19, Leviticus 11–12, Proverbs 24
March 7 - Matthew 11:20–30, Leviticus 13, Proverbs 25
March 8 - Matthew 12:1–21, Leviticus 14, Proverbs 26
March 9 - Matthew 12:22–50, Leviticus 15–16, Proverbs 27
March 10 - Matthew 13:1–23, Leviticus 17–18, Proverbs 28
March 11 - Matthew 13:24–58, Leviticus 19, Proverbs 29
March 12 - Matthew 14:1–21, Leviticus 20–21, Proverbs 30
March 13 - Matthew 14:22–36, Leviticus 22–23, Proverbs 31
March 14 - Matthew 15:1–20, Leviticus 24–25, Ecclesiastes 1:1–11
March 15 - Matthew 15:21–39, Leviticus 26–27, Ecclesiastes
    1:12–2:26
March 16 - Matthew 16, Numbers 1–2, Ecclesiastes 3:1–15
March 17 - Matthew 17, Numbers 3–4, Ecclesiastes 3:16–4:16
March 18 - Matthew 18:1–20, Numbers 5–6, Ecclesiastes 5
March 19 - Matthew 18:21–35, Numbers 7–8, Ecclesiastes 6
March 20 - Matthew 19:1–15, Numbers 9–10, Ecclesiastes 7
March 21 - Matthew 19:16–30, Numbers 11–12, Ecclesiastes 8
March 22 - Matthew 20:1–16, Numbers 13–14, Ecclesiastes
    9:1–12
March 23 - Matthew 20:17–34, Numbers 15–16, Ecclesiastes
    9:13–10:20
March 24 - Matthew 21:1–27, Numbers 17–18, Ecclesiastes
    11:1–8
March 25 - Matthew 21:28–46, Numbers 19–20, Ecclesiastes
    11:9–12:14
March 26 - Matthew 22:1–22, Numbers 21,
    Song of Solomon 1:1–2:7

March 27 - Matthew 22:23–46, Numbers 22:1–40,
        Song of Solomon 2:8-3:5
March 28 - Matthew 23:1–12, Numbers 22:41–23:26,
        Song of Solomon 3:6–5:1
March 29 - Matthew 23:13–39, Numbers 23:27–24:25,
        Song of Solomon 5:2–6:3
March 30 - Matthew 24:1–31, Numbers 25–27,
        Song of Solomon 6:4–8:4
March 31 - Matthew 24:32–51, Numbers 28–29,
        Song of Solomon 8:5–14

Bible Readings for April

April 1 - Matthew 25:1–30, Numbers 30–31, Job 1
April 2 - Matthew 25:31–46, Numbers 32–34, Job 2
April 3 - Matthew 26:1–25, Numbers 35–36, Job 3
April 4 - Matthew 26:26–46, Deuteronomy 1–2, Job 4
April 5 - Matthew 26:47–75, Deuteronomy 3–4, Job 5
April 6 - Matthew 27:1–31, Deuteronomy 5–6, Job 6
April 7 - Matthew 27:32–66, Deuteronomy 7–8, Job 7
April 8 - Matthew 28, Deuteronomy 9–10, Job 8
April 9 - Acts 1, Deuteronomy 11–12, Job 9
April 10 - Acts 2:1–13, Deuteronomy 13–14, Job 10
April 11 - Acts 2:14–47, Deuteronomy 15–16, Job 11
April 12 - Acts 3, Deuteronomy 17–18, Job 12
April 13 - Acts 4:1–22, Deuteronomy 19–20, Job 13
April 14 - Acts 4:23–37, Deuteronomy 21–22, Job 14
April 15 - Acts 5:1–16, Deuteronomy 23–24, Job 15
April 16 - Acts 5:17–42, Deuteronomy 25–27, Job 16
April 17 - Acts 6, Deuteronomy 28, Job 17
April 18 - Acts 7:1–22, Deuteronomy 29–30, Job 18
April 19 - Acts 7:23–60, Deuteronomy 31–32, Job 19
April 20 - Acts 8:1–25, Deuteronomy 33–34, Job 20
April 21 - Acts 8:26–40, Joshua 1–2, Job 21
April 22 - Acts 9:1–25, Joshua 3:1–5:1, Job 22
April 23 - Acts 9:26–43, Joshua 5:2–6:27, Job 23
April 24 - Acts 10:1–33, Joshua 7–8, Job 24
April 25 - Acts 10:34–48, Joshua 9–10, Job 25
April 26 - Acts 11:1–18, Joshua 11–12, Job 26
April 27 - Acts 11:19–30, Joshua 13–14, Job 27
April 28 - Acts 12, Joshua 15–17, Job 28
April 29 - Acts 13:1–25, Joshua 18–19, Job 29
April 30 - Acts 13:26–52, Joshua 20–21, Job 30

Bible Readings for May

May 1 - Acts 14, Joshua 22, Job 31
May 2 - Acts 15:1–21, Joshua 23–24, Job 32
May 3 - Acts 15:22–41, Judges 1, Job 33
May 4 - Acts 16:1–15, Judges 2–3, Job 34
May 5 - Acts 16:16–40, Judges 4–5, Job 35
May 6 - Acts 17:1–15, Judges 6, Job 36
May 7 - Acts 17:16–34, Judges 7–8, Job 37
May 8 - Acts 18, Judges 9, Job 38
May 9 - Acts 19:1–20, Judges 10:1–11:33, Job 39
May 10 - Acts 19:21–41, Judges 11:34–12:15, Job 40
May 11 - Acts 20:1–16, Judges 13, Job 41
May 12 - Acts 20:17–38, Judges 14–15, Job 42
May 13 - Acts 21:1–36, Judges 16, Psalm 42
May 14 - Acts 21:37–22:29, Judges 17–18, Psalm 43
May 15 - Acts 22:30–23:22, Judges 19, Psalm 44
May 16 - Acts 23:23–24:9, Judges 20, Psalm 45
May 17 - Acts 24:10–27, Judges 21, Psalm 46
May 18 - Acts 25, Ruth 1–2, Psalm 47
May 19 - Acts 26:1–18, Ruth 3–4, Psalm 48
May 20 - Acts 26:19–32, 1 Samuel 1:1–2:10, Psalm 49
May 21 - Acts 27:1–12, 1 Samuel 2:11–36, Psalm 50
May 22 - Acts 27:13–44, 1 Samuel 3, Psalm 51
May 23 - Acts 28:1–16, 1 Samuel 4–5, Psalm 52
May 24 - Acts 28:17–31, 1 Samuel 6–7, Psalm 53
May 25 - Romans 1:1–15, 1 Samuel 8, Psalm 54
May 26 - Romans 1:16–32, 1 Samuel 9:1–10:16, Psalm 55
May 27 - Romans 2:1–3:8, 1 Samuel 10:17–11:15, Psalm 56
May 28 - Romans 3:9–31, 1 Samuel 12, Psalm 57
May 29 - Romans 4, 1 Samuel 13, Psalm 58
May 30 - Romans 5, 1 Samuel 14, Psalm 59
May 31 - Romans 6, 1 Samuel 15, Psalm 60

Bible Readings for June

June 1 - Romans 7, 1 Samuel 16, Psalm 61
June 2 - Romans 8 1 Samuel 17:1–54, Psalm 62
June 3 - Romans 9:1–29, 1 Samuel 17:55–18:30, Psalm 63
June 4 - Romans 9:30–10:21, 1 Samuel 19, Psalm 64
June 5 - Romans 11:1–24, 1 Samuel 20, Psalm 65
June 6 - Romans 11:25–36, 1 Samuel 21–22, Psalm 66
June 7 - Romans 12, 1 Samuel 23–24, Psalm 67
June 8 - Romans 13, 1 Samuel 25, Psalm 68
June 9 - Romans 14, 1 Samuel 26, Psalm 69
June 10 - Romans 15:1–13, 1 Samuel 27–28, Psalm 70
June 11 - Romans 15:14–33, 1 Samuel 29–31, Psalm 71
June 12 - Romans 16, 2 Samuel 1, Psalm 72
June 13 - Mark 1:1–20, 2 Samuel 2:1–3:1, Daniel 1
June 14 - Mark 1:21–45, 2 Samuel 3:2–39, Daniel 2:1–23
June 15 - Mark 2, 2 Samuel 4–5, Daniel 2:24–49
June 16 - Mark 3:1–19, 2 Samuel 6, Daniel 3
June 17 - Mark 3:20–35, 2 Samuel 7–8, Daniel 4
June 18 - Mark 4:1–20, 2 Samuel 9–10, Daniel 5
June 19 - Mark 4:21–41, 2 Samuel 11–12, Daniel 6
June 20 - Mark 5:1–20, 2 Samuel 13, Daniel 7
June 21 - Mark 5:21–43, 2 Samuel 14, Daniel 8
June 22 - Mark 6:1–29, 2 Samuel 15, Daniel 9
June 23 - Mark 6:30–56, 2 Samuel 16, Daniel 10
June 24 - Mark 7:1–13, 2 Samuel 17, Daniel 11:1–19
June 25 - Mark 7:14–37, 2 Samuel 18, Daniel 11:20–45
June 26 - Mark 8:1–21, 2 Samuel 19, Daniel 12
June 27 - Mark 8:22–9:1, 2 Samuel 20–21, Hosea 1:1–2:1
June 28 - Mark 9:2–50, 2 Samuel 22, Hosea 2:2–23
June 29 - Mark 10:1–31, 2 Samuel 23, Hosea 3
June 30 - Mark 10:32–52, 2 Samuel 24, Hosea 4:1–11

Bible Readings for July

July 1 - Mark 11:1–14, 1 Kings 1, Hosea 4:12–5:4
July 2 - Mark 11:15–33, 1 Kings 2, Hosea 5:5–15
July 3 - Mark 12:1–27, 1 Kings 3, Hosea 6:1–7:2
July 4 - Mark 12:28–44, 1 Kings 4-5, Hosea 7:3–16
July 5 - Mark 13:1–13, 1 Kings 6, Hosea 8
July 6 - Mark 13:14–37, 1 Kings 7, Hosea 9:1–16
July 7 - Mark 14:1–31, 1 Kings 8, Hosea 9:17–10:15
July 8 - Mark 14:32–72, 1 Kings 9, Hosea 11:1–11
July 9 - Mark 15:1–20, 1 Kings 10, Hosea 11:12–12:14
July 10 - Mark 15:21–47, 1 Kings 11, Hosea 13
July 11 - Mark 16, 1 Kings 12:1–31, Hosea 14
July 12 - 1 Corinthians 1:1–17, 1 Kings 12:32–13:34, Joel 1
July 13 - 1 Corinthians 1:18–31, 1 Kings 14, Joel 2:1–11
July 14 - 1 Corinthians 2, 1 Kings 15:1–32, Joel 2:12–32
July 15 - 1 Corinthians 3, 1 Kings 15:33–16:34, Joel 3
July 16 - 1 Corinthians 4, 1 Kings 17, Amos 1
July 17 - 1 Corinthians 5, 1 Kings 18, Amos 2:1–3:2
July 18 - 1 Corinthians 6, 1 Kings 19, Amos 3:3–4:3
July 19 - 1 Corinthians 7:1–24, 1 Kings 20, Amos 4:4–13
July 20 - 1 Corinthians 7:25–40, 1 Kings 21, Amos 5
July 21 - 1 Corinthians 8, 1 Kings 22, Amos 6
July 22 - 1 Corinthians 9, 2 Kings 1–2, Amos 7
July 23 - 1 Corinthians 10, 2 Kings 3, Amos 8
July 24 - 1 Corinthians 11:1–16, 2 Kings 4, Amos 9
July 25 - 1 Corinthians 11:17–34, 2 Kings 5, Obadiah
July 26 - 1 Corinthians 12, 2 Kings 6:1–7:2, Jonah 1
July 27 - 1 Corinthians 13, 2 Kings 7:3–20, Jonah 2
July 28 - 1 Corinthians 14:1–25, 2 Kings 8, Jonah 3
July 29 - 1 Corinthians 14:26–40, 2 Kings 9, Jonah 4
July 30 - 1 Corinthians 15:1–34, 2 Kings 10, Micah 1
July 31 - 1 Corinthians 15:35–58, 2 Kings 11, Micah 2

Bible Readings for August

August 1 - 1 Corinthians 16, 2 Kings 12–13, Micah 3
August 2 - 2 Corinthians 1:1–2:4, 2 Kings 14, Micah 4:1–5:1
August 3 - 2 Corinthians 2:5–3:18, 2 Kings 15–16, Micah 5:2–15
August 4 - 2 Corinthians 4:1–5:10, 2 Kings 17, Micah 6
August 5 - 2 Corinthians 5:11–6:13, 2 Kings 18, Micah 7
August 6 - 2 Corinthians 6:14–7:16, 2 Kings 19, Nahum 1
August 7 - 2 Corinthians 8, 2 Kings 20–21, Nahum 2
August 8 - 2 Corinthians 9, 2 Kings 22:1–23:35, Nahum 3
August 9 - 2 Corinthians 10, 2 Kings 23:36–24:20, Habakkuk 1
August 10 - 2 Corinthians 11, 2 Kings 25, Habakkuk 2
August 11 - 2 Corinthians 12, 1 Chronicles 1–2, Habakkuk 3
August 12 - 2 Corinthians 13, 1 Chronicles 3–4, Zephaniah 1
August 13 - John 1:1–18, 1 Chronicles 5–6, Zephaniah 2
August 14 - John 1:19–34, 1 Chronicles 7–8, Zephaniah 3
August 15 - John 1:35–51, 1 Chronicles 9, Haggai 1–2
August 16 - John 2, 1 Chronicles 10–11, Zechariah 1
August 17 - John 3:1–21, 1 Chronicles 12, Zechariah 2
August 18 - John 3:22–36, 1 Chronicles 13–14, Zechariah 3
August 19 - John 4:1–26, 1 Chronicles 15:1–16:6, Zechariah 4
August 20 - John 4:27–42, 1 Chronicles 16:7–43, Zechariah 5
August 21 - John 4:43–54, 1 Chronicles 17, Zechariah 6
August 22 - John 5:1–18, 1 Chronicles 18–19, Zechariah 7
August 23 - John 5:19–47, 1 Chronicles 20:1–22:1, Zechariah 8
August 24 - John 6:1–21, 1 Chronicles 22:2–23:32, Zechariah 9
August 25 - John 6:22–59, 1 Chronicles 24, Zechariah 10
August 26 - John 6:60–71, 1 Chronicles 25–26, Zechariah 11
August 27 - John 7:1–24, 1 Chronicles 27–28, Zechariah 12
August 28 - John 7:25–52, 1 Chronicles 29, Zechariah 13
August 29 - John 8:1–20, 2 Chronicles 1:1–2:16, Zechariah 14
August 30 - John 8:21–47, 2 Chronicles 2:17–5:1, Malachi 1:1–2:9
August 31 - John 8:48–59, 2 Chronicles 5:2–14, Malachi 2:10–16

Bible Readings for September

September 1 - John 9:1–23, 2 Chronicles 6, Malachi 2:17–3:18
September 2 - John 9:24–41, 2 Chronicles 7, Malachi 4
September 3 - John 10:1–21, 2 Chronicles 8, Psalm 73
September 4 - John 10:22–42, 2 Chronicles 9, Psalm 74
September 5 - John 11:1–27, 2 Chronicles 10–11, Psalm 75
September 6 - John 11:28–57, 2 Chronicles 12–13, Psalm 76
September 7 - John 12:1–26, 2 Chronicles 14–15, Psalm 77
September 8 - John 12:27–50, 2 Chronicles 16–17, Psalm 78:1-20
September 9 - John 13:1–20, 2 Chronicles 18, Psalm 78:21–37
September 10 - John 13:21–38, 2 Chronicles 19, Psalm 78:38–55
September 11 - John 14:1–14, 2 Chronicles 20:1–21:1,
        Psalm 78:56–72
September 12 - John 14:15–31, 2 Chronicles 21:2–22:12,
        Psalm 79
September 13 - John 15:1–16:4, 2 Chronicles 23, Psalm 80
September 14 - John 16:4–33, 2 Chronicles 24, Psalm 81
September 15 - John 17, 2 Chronicles 25, Psalm 82
September 16 - John 18:1–18, 2 Chronicles 26, Psalm 83
September 17 - John 18:19–38, 2 Chronicles 27–28, Psalm 84
September 18 - John 18:38–19:16, 2 Chronicles 29, Psalm 85
September 19 - John 19:16–42, 2 Chronicles 30, Psalm 86
September 20 - John 20:1–18, 2 Chronicles 31, Psalm 87
September 21 - John 20:19–31, 2 Chronicles 32, Psalm 88
September 22 - John 21, 2 Chronicles 33, Psalm 89:1–18
September 23 - 1 John 1, 2 Chronicles 34, Psalm 89:19–37
September 24 - 1 John 2, 2 Chronicles 35, Psalm 89:38–52
September 25 - 1 John 3, 2 Chronicles 36, Psalm 90
September 26 - 1 John 4, Ezra 1–2, Psalm 91
September 27 - 1 John 5, Ezra 3–4, Psalm 92
September 28 - 2 John, Ezra 5–6, Psalm 93
September 29 - 3 John, Ezra 7–8, Psalm 94
September 30 - Jude, Ezra 9–10, Psalm 95

Bible Readings for October

October 1 - Revelation 1, Nehemiah 1–2, Psalm 96
October 2 - Revelation 2, Nehemiah 3, Psalm 97
October 3 - Revelation 3, Nehemiah 4, Psalm 98
October 4 - Revelation 4, Nehemiah 5:1–7:4, Psalm 99
October 5 - Revelation 5, Nehemiah 7:5–8:12, Psalm 100
October 6 - Revelation 6, Nehemiah 8:13–9:37, Psalm 101
October 7 - Revelation 7, Nehemiah 9:38–10:39, Psalm 102
October 8 - Revelation 8, Nehemiah 11, Psalm 103
October 9 - Revelation 9, Nehemiah 12, Psalm 104:1–23
October 10 - Revelation 10, Nehemiah 13, Psalm 104:24–35
October 11 - Revelation 11, Esther 1, Psalm 105:1–25
October 12 - Revelation 12, Esther 2, Psalm 105:26–45
October 13 - Revelation 13, Esther 3–4, Psalm 106:1–23
October 14 - Revelation 14, Esther 5:1–6:13, Psalm 106:24–48
October 15 - Revelation 15, Esther 6:14–8:17, Psalm 107:1–22
October 16 - Revelation 16, Esther 9–10, Psalm 107:23–43
October 17 - Revelation 17, Isaiah 1–2, Psalm 108
October 18 - Revelation 18, Isaiah 3–4, Psalm 109:1–19
October 19 - Revelation 19, Isaiah 5–6, Psalm 109:20–31
October 20 - Revelation 20, Isaiah 7–8, Psalm 110
October 21 - Revelation 21–22, Isaiah 9–10, Psalm 111
October 22 - 1 Thessalonians 1, Isaiah 11–13, Psalm 112
October 23 - 1 Thessalonians 2:1–16, Isaiah 14–16,
        Psalm 113
October 24 - 1 Thessalonians 2:17–3:13, Isaiah 17–19, Psalm 114
October 25 - 1 Thessalonians 4, Isaiah 20–22, Psalm 115
October 26 - 1 Thessalonians 5, Isaiah 23–24, Psalm 116
October 27 - 2 Thessalonians 1, Isaiah 25–26, Psalm 117
October 28 - 2 Thessalonians 2, Isaiah 27–28, Psalm 118
October 29 - 2 Thessalonians 3, Isaiah 29–30, Psalm 119:1–32
October 30 - 1 Timothy 1, Isaiah 31–33, Psalm 119:33–64
October 31 - 1 Timothy 2, Isaiah 34–35, Psalm 119:65–96

Bible Readings for November

November 1 - 1 Timothy 3, Isaiah 36–37, Psalm 119:97–120
November 2 - 1 Timothy 4, Isaiah 38–39, Psalm 119:121–144
November 3 - 1 Timothy 5:1–22, Jeremiah 1–2,
           Psalm 119:145–176
November 4 - 1 Timothy 5:23–6:21, Jeremiah 3–4, Psalm 120
November 5 - 2 Timothy 1, Jeremiah 5–6, Psalm 121
November 6 - 2 Timothy 2, Jeremiah 7–8, Psalm 122
November 7 - 2 Timothy 3, Jeremiah 9–10, Psalm 123
November 8 - 2 Timothy 4, Jeremiah 11–12, Psalm 124
November 9 - Titus 1, Jeremiah 13–14, Psalm 125
November 10 - Titus 2, Jeremiah 15–16, Psalm 126
November 11 - Titus 3, Jeremiah 17–18, Psalm 127
November 12 - Philemon, Jeremiah 19–20, Psalm 128
November 13 - James 1, Jeremiah 21–22, Psalm 129
November 14 - James 2, Jeremiah 23–24, Psalm 130
November 15 - James 3, Jeremiah 25–26, Psalm 131
November 16 - James 4, Jeremiah 27–28, Psalm 132
November 17 - James 5, Jeremiah 29–30, Psalm 133
November 18 - 1 Peter 1, Jeremiah 31–32, Psalm 134
November 19 - 1 Peter 2, Jeremiah 33–34, Psalm 135
November 20 - 1 Peter 3, Jeremiah 35–36, Psalm 136
November 21 - 1 Peter 4, Jeremiah 37–38, Psalm 137
November 22 - 1 Peter 5, Jeremiah 39–40, Psalm 138
November 23 - 2 Peter 1, Jeremiah 41–42, Psalm 139
November 24 - 2 Peter 2, Jeremiah 43–44, Psalm 140
November 25 - 2 Peter 3, Jeremiah 45–46, Psalm 141
November 26 - Galatians 1, Jeremiah 47–48, Psalm 142
November 27 - Galatians 2, Jeremiah 49–50, Psalm 143
November 28 - Galatians 3:1–18, Jeremiah 51–52, Psalm 144
November 29 - Galatians 3:19–4:20, Lamentations 1–2, Psalm 145
November 30 - Galatians 4:21–31, Lamentations 3–4, Psalm 146

Bible Readings for December

December 1 - Galatians 5:1–15, Lamentations 5, Psalm 147
December 2 - Galatians 5:16–26, Ezekiel 1, Psalm 148
December 3 - Galatians 6, Ezekiel 2–3, Psalm 149
December 4 - Ephesians 1, Ezekiel 4–5, Psalm 150
December 5 - Ephesians 2, Ezekiel 6–7, Isaiah 40
December 6 - Ephesians 3, Ezekiel 8–9, Isaiah 41
December 7 - Ephesians 4:1–16, Ezekiel 10–11, Isaiah 42
December 8 - Ephesians 4:17–32, Ezekiel 12–13, Isaiah 43
December 9 - Ephesians 5:1–20, Ezekiel 14–15, Isaiah 44
December 10 - Ephesians 5:21–33, Ezekiel 16, Isaiah 45
December 11 - Ephesians 6, Ezekiel 17, Isaiah 46
December 12 - Philippians 1:1–11, Ezekiel 18, Isaiah 47
December 13 - Philippians 1:12–30, Ezekiel 19, Isaiah 48
December 14 - Philippians 2:1–11, Ezekiel 20, Isaiah 49
December 15 - Philippians 2:12–30, Ezekiel 21–22,
          Isaiah 50
December 16 - Philippians 3, Ezekiel 23, Isaiah 51
December 17 - Philippians 4, Ezekiel 24, Isaiah 52
December 18 - Colossians 1:1–23, Ezekiel 25–26, Isaiah 53
December 19 - Colossians 1:24–2:19, Ezekiel 27–28,
          Isaiah 54
December 20 - Colossians 2:20–3:17, Ezekiel 29–30,
          Isaiah 55
December 21 - Colossians 3:18–4:18, Ezekiel 31–32,
          Isaiah 56
December 22 - Luke 1:1–25, Ezekiel 33, Isaiah 57
December 23 - Luke 1:26–56, Ezekiel 34, Isaiah 58
December 24 - Luke 1:57–80, Ezekiel 35–36, Isaiah 59
December 25 - Luke 2:1–20, Ezekiel 37, Isaiah 60
December 26 - Luke 2:21–52, Ezekiel 38–39, Isaiah 61
December 27 - Luke 3:1–20, Ezekiel 40–41, Isaiah 62
December 28 - Luke 3:21–38, Ezekiel 42–43, Isaiah 63
December 29 - Luke 4:1–30, Ezekiel 44–45, Isaiah 64

Notes

_____

_____

_____

_____

_____

_____

_____

_____

_____

_____

_____

_____

_____

_____

Notes

_____

_____

_____

_____

_____

_____

_____

_____

_____

_____

_____

_____

_____